"*Living and Loving after Betrayal* offers a strong rope out of the quicksand of misery and despair that couples sink into after a betrayal. Stosny's guide to healing the heartache of betrayal is the most helpful I have seen in twenty-five years of clinical practice."

> —**Ronald J. Coughlin, EdD**, licensed psychologist with twenty-five years in full-time private practice

"Since a pain-free life isn't possible, we need to understand and follow the wisdom provided in *Living and Loving after Betrayal*. Stosny, one of today's most highly respected relationship experts, understands how to grow and have a more satisfying life after being deeply hurt by others. This is a deceptively simple tool kit for effectively handling the full range of relationship disappointments and heartaches."

> —**Jon Carlson, PsyD, EdD**, distinguished professor in the Division of Psychology & Counseling, Governors State University

"This is a remarkably wise and compassionate guide to healing from intimate betrayal. It will help you recover the best of yourself rather than remain stuck in anger or anxiety. I will ask my clients to read this book and I will give it to loved ones who are on a healing journey."

> —**William J. Doherty, PhD**, professor and director of the Minnesota Couples on the Brink Project at the University of Minnesota, and author of *Take Back Your Marriage.*

"Stosny has broken new ground for individuals moving forward from any type of betrayal or violation of the intimate bonds of relationships. He takes the reader beyond hurt, even beyond healing, into the area of personal mastery by way of compassion. This book is a must read for anyone who has felt the pain and disappointment of a once-trusted relationship."

—**Pat Love, EdD**, coauthor of *How to Improve Your Marriage without Talking about It* and *Never Be Lonely Again*

"This excellent book addresses an often-overlooked aspect of healing from betrayal, and that is self-healing. When people get hurt, their attention usually turns to the perpetrator of the hurt—one's partner. But part of the real work that needs to be done is on one's self.

"If you have felt the devastating effects of betrayal, this must-read book will help restore your inner resilience and faith in yourself so you can get through the difficult periods and thrive beyond them. Stosny's workbook-like exercises help you apply what you're learning to your own unique situation. You'll feel like you have a personal coach guiding you to better times!"

—**Michele Weiner-Davis**, author of *Divorce Busting* and *The Sex-Starved Marriage*

LIVING &
LOVING
after
BETRAYAL

How to Heal *from* Emotional Abuse, Deceit, Infidelity, *and* Chronic Resentment

STEVEN STOSNY, PhD

New Harbinger Publications, Inc.

Distributed in Canada by Raincoast Books

Copyright © 2013 by Steven Stosny
New Harbinger Publications, Inc.
5674 Shattuck Avenue
Oakland, CA 94609
www.newharbinger.com

Cover design by Amy Shoup
Acquired by Melissa Kirk
Edited by Susan LaCroix

Library of Congress Cataloging in Publication Data

Stosny, Steven.
  Living and loving after betrayal : how to heal from emotional abuse, deceit, infidelity, and chronic resentment / Steven Stosny, PhD.
      pages cm
  Includes bibliographical references.
  ISBN 978-1-60882-752-7 (pbk. : alk. paper) -- ISBN 978-1-60882-753-4 (pdf e-book) -- ISBN 978-1-60882-754-1 (epub) 1. Trust. 2. Betrayal. 3. Intimacy (Psychology) 4. Interpersonal conflict. 5. Interpersonal relations. 6. Couples--Psychology. I. Title.
  BF575.T7S76 2013
  158.2--dc23

                              2013011797

Printed in the United States of America

15   14   13

10   9   8   7   6   5   4   3   2   1   First printing

To my thousands of clients who have shown the awesome courage to heal and grow from the depths of relationship betrayal.

And, as always, to my mother, who overcame every form of intimate betrayal to become a compassionate, loving, and powerful person.

Contents

Part III Loving Again

Part IV Rebuilding a Betrayed Relationship

Introduction

If you have felt betrayed by a lover in a committed relationship, you know all too well that intimate betrayal is a pain unlike any other, striking at the core of our capacity to trust and love. This extraordinarily harsh and lingering pain almost invariably overflows into other areas of life. Work efficiency plummets for most who suffer its sting. Some feel unable to resume their normal level of caring behavior in any relationship, including those with friends, parents, and children. Many are left feeling unworthy of love. Most endure long periods of dull ache or depressed mood, punctuated by torrents of anger, shame, guilt, anxiety, resentment, and grief.

The destructive force and lasting effects of intimate betrayal come from its violation of the implicit promise that gives us the courage to love in the first place: the promise that no matter what happens, the person you love and trust will care about your well-being and never intentionally hurt you.

These two key elements classify the types of intimate betrayal. Behaviors that *intentionally hurt* include most emotional abuse, verbal aggression, and domestic violence. Failure to care about your well-being covers most deceit, infidelity, covert misuse of communal resources, continual resentment, anger, criticism, stonewalling, and other isolating or hurtful behaviors.

Think Healing and Growth, Not Labels

For the purposes of this book, I'll define emotional betrayal as anything that left you feeling betrayed, hurt, angry, and distrusting, with lingering aftereffects of painful memories. That said, labeling specific behaviors as "betrayal" or "abusive" or "deceitful" is not the purpose of this book, and not just because labels tend to oversimplify complex patterns of behavior and the contexts in which they occur. More importantly, you should not be made to feel that you must explain your experience or justify your pain to qualify for a certain label. Trying to fit your circumstance into convenient labels would keep you focused on the extent and causes of your injuries rather than healing and outgrowing them; that is to say, it would embed the footprints of betrayal in your heart and soul. You've probably had arguments with your betrayer concerning labels of his behavior—you saw it one way and he denied, minimized, evaded, or blamed. Such arguments are as fruitless as they are frustrating. Worse, they obscure the most vital issue: your pain, which seemed to get lost in disputes over behavioral labels and characterizations.

Let's declare right from the start: You do not have to justify your hurt or fit it into any kind of category. You don't have to characterize your partner's behavior with labels you get from a book. All that matters is that it hurt you, and you deserve to focus your enormous emotional resources on the difficult task of healing, recovery, and growth. This book will give you the courage and skill to do so.

Get Out of the Hole First

I will not use the pages of this book to explore details about the specific kinds of intimate betrayal and how they occur. Chances are you have done more than enough of that, for there is a tendency to become preoccupied with the minutiae of how we're mistreated, which only distracts from the healing process.

Neither will I speculate about the motivations of your faithless partner, for there is an equally ominous tendency to live too much in the head of the betrayer, which can easily make you lose a sense of who you are. When it comes to recovering from intimate betrayal, it's best to get out of the hole before speculating about how you got into it. Accordingly, the book will focus on healing the wounds common to all forms of betrayal and outgrowing the negative effects of your partner's failings, regardless of what may or may not have caused them.

Should you decide to repair your relationship with your betrayer, I am convinced that you must go through the individual healing process put forth in this book before you try to repair the relationship. Otherwise, you may end up sacrificing personal healing and growth in attempts to save a damaged union, which cannot be meaningfully repaired as long as there are open wounds. Accordingly, chapters on relationship repair come at the very end of the book.

Most of the book centers on ways to overcome the many barriers to healing and on forging a path through the numerous brambles that inhibit growth and obscure full recovery.

Awe and Courage

I have been awed by the sheer courage of so many of the clients I've had the privilege to work with in my many years of clinical practice.

Nearly 3,000 have more than healed the wounds of various forms of intimate betrayal; they have transcended all residual effects of their pain to become the emotionally open, fair-minded, and compassionate people they were meant to be. The human spirit is remarkably resilient and inspiring in its ability to grow beyond the scars of ill treatment.

As my clients have inspired me, I hope that this book will empower, encourage, and reassure you who have suffered. My work with people who have endured the worst kind of emotional pain has convinced me of this fact:

> *Determined focus on healing, growing, and creating a life that you deeply value is the only reliable way to heal from the past and prevent betrayal in the future.*

Style note: In an effort to avoid awkwardness in the use of complex pronouns, while trying to eliminate gender bias, I have endeavored to alternate the gender of personal pronouns.

Part I

The Start of Healing and Empowerment

The many forms of intimate betrayal are typically followed by a hor-rific roller-coaster ride of disturbing emotions. As if that weren't bad enough, the natural defenses to cope with sometimes unbearable pain will quite often, in the long run, serve to prolong the suffering, retard healing, and inhibit growth. This section of the book will offer a deeper understanding of pain, which evolved to keep us safe and well. It will show how to use the natural motivation of pain to heal, repair, and improve. Most important, it will show how to develop a "healing identity" that will help marshal all your intellectual, emotional, and spiritual resources for healing and growth.

CHAPTER 1

Footprints on the Heart and Soul

There are compelling biological reasons that intimate betrayal hurts so badly and is so hard to overcome. Love relationships are held together by deep emotional bonds that were crucial to the very survival of our species.

Most anthropologists agree that early humans could not have survived without strong emotional bonds that made us cooperate in food gathering and territorial defense. Not surprisingly, we have developed preverbal, prerational, automatic emotional reactions to behaviors and attitudes that threaten emotional bonds. These developed in our brains in prehistoric times, when to leave the kinship of the tribe meant certain death, by starvation or saber-toothed tiger. The reactions to intimate betrayal often include a vague feeling that you might die. The feeling is highly irrational, because it emanates from a primitive part of the brain, but it is nonetheless forceful and real. Indeed, most suicides follow attachment loss, as do most intimate homicides.

How It Hits You

Intimate betrayal upends your life in one of two ways: by sudden revelation or by gradual realization.

With deceit, embezzlement, and infidelity, you discover that your partner has lied, manipulated, stolen, or cheated. You may have guessed that something was amiss, but no amount of suspicion could mitigate the shock and hurt when struck by your partner's confession; an eyewitness account; uncovered e-mails, texts, or phone messages; or other incontrovertible evidence. You became aware in an instant that your life would never be the same.

Some faces of intimate betrayal, such as abuse or being forced to walk on eggshells to appease a partner who is chronically resentful, angry, critical, stonewalling, or self-obsessed, strike just as forcefully but as a more gradual realization of what your life has become. You may have tried for a long time to make the best of your partner's bad behavior—overlooked it, made excuses for it, or simply refused to identify it. Your instinct to adapt, cooperate, and trust would have benefited most relationships. Yet your noble efforts to preserve emotional bonds with your partner (and protect your children, if you have them) may have delayed recognition of the betrayal you have suffered.

The Floor of Security Crumbles

Whether it crashes upon you in revelation or seeps into consciousness via delayed realization, intimate betrayal snatches the floor of personal security from under you. Most of my clients describe the initial aftermath of revelation and realization as a kind of free fall, with no bottom in sight. Shock and disbelief are punctuated by waves of cruel self-doubt:

Was I attractive enough, smart enough, successful enough, interesting enough, present, attentive, caring, patient, or sacrificing enough?

The New Floor: Anger

Shock, disbelief, and self-doubt may have given way to intense anger that seems to course through your veins whenever you think of the betrayal, and you probably think of it often. The frightening uncertainty and utter powerlessness of the free-fall condition is why betrayal of any kind stimulates the most virulent form of anger. Betrayal and anger are typically inseparable, for a while. The reasons owe more to biology than to psychology.

A survival emotion common to all mammals, anger has potent analgesic and amphetamine components that temporarily numb pain and provide a surge of energy to overcome perceived threat. These effects empower animals to flee when vulnerable to threat, or to fight when flight is not possible. This is why the weakened tend to be skittish and the wounded become ferocious.

The same protective mechanism common to all mammals is activated by intimate betrayal. The surge of energy and pain-numbing qualities of anger temporarily ease powerlessness, self-doubt, and vulnerability.

High Risks in the Aftermath of Intimate Betrayal

Just about everyone drinks more alcohol after suffering attachment loss of any kind, including intimate betrayal. Although it's a cliché, "drowning your sorrows" after loss of attachment has considerable empirical support (Byrne, Raphael, Arnold, 1999; Wingood, DiClemente, and Raj 2000).

A more subtle kind of addictive trap afflicts even those who don't drink. The analgesic effect of anger temporarily relieves pain. That's why you swear when you bang your thumb hanging a picture. It's why athletes who get angry in the game can break a bone and not know it. It's why we get irritable when ill or in pain. Anything that relieves pain can become psychologically addictive or at least habituated, as the brain indelibly associates pain with whatever relieves it.

The greater addictive trap of anger comes from its amphetamine effect. Amphetamines—the "speed" drugs—provide a surge of energy, increased confidence, and a sense of power. Of course, the empowering effects are short-lived. The surge of energy, confidence, and power ends abruptly—in other words, you crash. Bouts of anger and resentment always drop you down lower than the point at which they picked you up; you get at least a little depressed or numb.

So here's the cycle that typically emerges in the aftermath of intimate betrayal: You think of the betrayal and get angry. The anger increases your energy, confidence, and sense of power. Then the amphetamine crash happens. The loss of energy and power create a void that is soon filled by self-doubt, depressed mood, or mere numbness. You think about the betrayal again, and get angry again, only to crash once again into low energy, self-doubt, depressed mood, or blank numbness. It won't take many repetitions of this cycle before your brain starts to think about the betrayal just so the anger will temporarily empower you against the terrible feelings that come after the amphetamine crash. It's not that you like thinking about it; it's just that thinking about it feels better than pain, depression, and numbness—at least as long as the adrenaline and analgesic effects of the anger last, which, for most people, isn't very long.

Few among us can tolerate a long roller-coaster ride of intense anger, depression, intense anger, depression, and so on. We tend to cut off the peaks and valleys by staying a little resentful all the time. Low-grade resentment keeps us from getting very angry and very depressed. It's understandable and natural to use resentment to avoid the anger-depression roller coaster that follows intimate betrayal. All of my betrayed clients had done so for quite some time before treatment. Their lives had become joyless drives to get things done. They did everything they needed to do—resentment has enough energy to keep you going—but they weren't interested in what they did and they enjoyed next to nothing. (Chronic resentment gobbles up the emotional energy that would normally go into interest and enjoyment.) They made more mistakes at work than usual, felt tense and irritable much of the time, and were not as sweet with their kids as they wanted to be. Loss of joy is only one of the many consequences of intimate betrayal.

The Most Unfair Thing about Intimate Betrayal

Anger evolved to provide a sense of power in the face of threat. It's the only emotion that mobilizes the entire central nervous system, every organ, every muscle group, and most of the metabolic system to generate the power required of the fight-or-flight response. More than any other internal experience, anger increases feelings of power. If loss of power were the problem in intimate betrayal, anger would be the answer. But the great pain of intimate betrayal has little to do with loss of power. Perceived loss of value is what causes your pain—you feel less lovable.

To recover, you must do what will make you feel more valuable and lovable, not temporarily more powerful. Yet defensive reactions to intimate betrayal—although perfectly natural and entirely justifiable—force you into reactive, narrow, and rigid perspectives that inhibit growth and further erode self-value. Allowed to run on automatic pilot, they will turn you into someone you're not.

Why It's So Hard to Be Yourself: Emotional Reactivity

An automatic, usually unconscious, gut-level response to negatively perceived events, situations, or people, emotional reactivity makes it very hard to be yourself after intimate betrayal. Almost anything—scenes in a movie, sporting events, e-mails, unexpected phone calls—can trigger memories or impressions of the betrayal and unleash intense emotions in reaction. The triggers can also generalize to nearly everyone with whom you interact. That is to say, a negative feeling in anyone else—for any reason—can stimulate emotional chaos or defensive shutdown in those who have suffered intimate betrayal. At its worst, high emotional reactivity hijacks your thoughts and feelings and too often makes you behave uncharacteristically. For example, my client Debbie, who had walked on eggshells for more than twenty years with a resentful and highly critical partner, suddenly burst into a whirlwind of anger and tears when a harried grocery checker sighed in response to her swiping her debit card backward. Debbie's embarrassment and remorse for her overreaction only made the public scene more awkward for her, the cashier, and shoppers in the long line behind her.

Debbie came to see me because of this and similar overreactions that were growing more frequent since her divorce. (Not all of her overreactions were acted out the way they were in the grocery store; some were internalized in the form of heightened tension or depressed mood.) Her previous therapist had worked with her to explore her feelings regarding her husband's betrayal—anger, resentment, shame, loss, abandonment, and so on—in the belief that unexplored and "stuffed" feelings caused her overreactions. When the overreactions increased in frequency, the therapist wanted her to take medication, which Debbie refused to do.

My approach to emotional healing is different. I assured Debbie that her feelings and reactions were normal and quite common. She didn't need to explore feelings that were a natural result of a sense of self scraped raw by intimate betrayal. Her high emotional reactivity was part of a larger defense system constructed to protect an understandably wounded heart from future harm. My therapeutic strategy was to build up her sense of personal value and empowerment and thereby render the heightened defensive system unnecessary.

Debbie's defensive reactions, like those of practically all my betrayed clients, had become habituated by the time I saw her. (Any mental activity repeated often will form a relatively inflexible sequence of neural firing in the brain—that is, a habit.) Once habits are formed, only new habits can replace them. Conditioning new mental, emotional, and behavioral habits is the foundation of my approach to healing and growth.

We'll return to Debbie later in the chapter. The point I want to emphasize here is that high emotional reactivity is not a problem of individual psychology. There was nothing wrong with Debbie, and there is nothing wrong with you, if you find yourself overreacting to life's minor irritations as well as its major challenges. High emotional reactivity—whether held in or acted out—results from a normal brain function known as *pattern matching*.

We hardly ever interact directly with our environment. The brain melds thoughts, memories, emotions, and behavioral impulses into thousands of neural "snapshots" and then selects one to "match" the current perception of the environment. This is normally an efficient way for it to function, because it conserves metabolically expensive conscious attention. That is, we exert the extra energy to pay attention only when something departs from our preconditioned "snapshots." You can walk into a room 100 times and not notice a lamp until, one day, it has been moved, and the pattern in your head no longer matches the appearance of the room.

Under normal conditions, the brain's pattern matching is pretty accurate, and we behave more or less "appropriately" most of the time. But intimate betrayal presents a special problem for pattern matching. The stronger the emotional component of the brain's neural snapshots, the less precise its matching process. That's especially true of the threat-related emotions—anger, fear, and disgust—which get priority processing in the brain. Seeing a cup of cream on the table can cause nausea in someone who has suffered food poisoning from bad meat or vegetables, as heightened sensitivity makes the cream, though unrelated to the rancid food that caused the poisoning, seem like a threat. A shadow on the wall can send a rape or mugging victim into fits of discomfort or terror, even though shadows routinely move on walls. A car backfiring, which sounds nothing like combat, can nevertheless trigger reality-shattering flashbacks in war veterans. If a past lover once cheated on you, a glow in the cheek of your present one can arouse anger, jealousy, and anxiety. In short, after intimate betrayal, your brain temporarily perceives the world to be more threatening than it really is. This change in perception is due to a normal brain function, not your personal psychology.

Another way to understand high emotional reactivity is to appreciate that your brain evolved as a "better safe than sorry" system. We did not descend from early humans who *under*estimated threat, who thought they didn't have to be extra careful after a brush with a saber-toothed tiger. We're descendant from the ones who *over*estimated threat and occasionally mistook shadows on the rocks—and sometimes fellow cave dwellers—for menacing beasts. When the grocery cashier sighed at Debbie's mistake with the credit card machine, he seemed, through the lens of her "better safe than sorry" defense system, to be the shadow of a saber-toothed tiger.

Overcoming Emotional Reactivity

This might sound strange coming from an experienced therapist specializing in emotion regulation, but the best way to overcome emotional reactivity is to make a determination to act on your values more than your feelings. (Your values are those beliefs and personal qualities that are most important to you. For instance, you might value being a supportive, nurturing mother or an honest and loyal friend.) After intimate betrayal, feelings tend to be confusing, contradictory, and, of course, highly reactive. More to the point, they are less about the person you truly are and more about defensive reactions to your environment. (Remember, your environment seems more dangerous in the aftermath of intimate betrayal, because the brain's pattern matching has become temporarily less accurate, in its "better safe than sorry" mode.) Acting on feelings will make you behave uncharacteristically, if not in ways that seem alien to you—which is what happened to Debbie and to many others like her. In contrast, your values represent who you truly are and what is most important to you, regardless of what occurs in your environment.

Acting on your values will change your feelings—if not immediately, in fairly short order—as you begin to feel more authentic, with less guilt, shame, anxiety, anger, and resentment. However, the converse is not true. If you act on your feelings, you run the risk of getting lost in the vicissitudes of temporary emotional states that will make you violate your deeper values and cause more guilt, shame, anxiety, anger, and resentment. For example, your betrayer almost certainly acted on her feelings in violation of her deeper values. The choice to act on feelings over values caused the betrayal.

A few crucial differences between feelings and values will make the better motivational choice obvious. Feelings are:

- more about what you're experiencing than who you are

- more reactive to the environment

- greatly influenced by physiological states (fatigue, hunger, thirst, body temperature, or illness)

- highly habituated—automatically stimulated by mere similarities with past experience

- transitory—coming and going within minutes, provided you don't amplify, magnify, and prolong them by trying to "validate" or "justify" them

In contrast, values are:

- more about you than what you're experiencing

- far less reactive to the environment

- far less influenced by physiological states

- consistent over time

After suffering intimate betrayal, it can be difficult to think in terms of deeper values, simply because the betrayal has made you consistently underestimate your personal value, strengths, and resilience. That was clearly Debbie's state when we started our first session. The key to her recovery was to begin thinking and acting in accordance with the person she truly is, beneath the pain and emotional reactivity she experienced.

Use the exercise below as a guide to act consistently according to your deeper values. The purpose of the exercise is to develop a repertoire of behaviors that will reinforce your deeper values and provide an automatic sense of authenticity.

A word of caution: Do not use the exercise to develop a way to relate to your betrayer—not yet, anyway. It's best to use relationships with fewer complications to begin the healing process. The optimal strategy for any kind of skill acquisition is to practice in relatively low-stress situations, until the skill becomes habituated, at which point you gradually increase the stress under which is it practiced. That's why you don't start swimming lessons in the ocean during a storm or make your first attempt at driving a car in speeding highway traffic. It's why the army doesn't put new recruits into combat without many weeks of basic training.

I've offered as examples in the "I am" column below those responses that Debbie and most of my clients have identified. Please list the qualities that correspond to your deepest values—for example, compassionate, protective, appreciative, loyal to loved ones, and so on. For each quality you identify, state a behavior that will reinforce that value. For example, if you choose "I am compassionate," a corresponding behavior could be "I will try to understand my loved ones' perspectives and try to find something in their motivations to sympathize with, especially when I disagree with them or want them to change their behavior."

A Crucial Note for All Exercises

The exercises in this book will not ask you to make mere "affirmations." Healing and growth require behavioral commitments to a new way of seeing yourself and the world. They do not arise miraculously from simple statements or temporary changes in feelings. There is a hierarchy of neurological change. Thinking repeatedly about something forges neural connections. Repeatedly imagining something in detail forges stronger connections. Thinking, imagining, and practicing behavior produces the most lasting change. You can start out just thinking in ways that promote healing and growth, but what you write in these exercises must be enacted in specific behaviors at some point, to accomplish full healing and growth.

VALUE-BEHAVIOR EXERCISE

On a blank sheet of paper, draw a vertical line separating it into two columns. In the first column, list your values, starting with "I am" (for example, "I am compassionate to loved ones"). Then, in the second column, list examples of how you will reinforce those values, starting with "I will" (for example, "I will try to understand my loved ones' perspectives and try to find something in their motivations to sympathize with, especially when I disagree with them or I want them to change their behavior"). List any number of values in the column on the left ("I am fair," "I am responsible," "I am appreciative of loved ones," and so on) and follow each with a corresponding action in the column on the right.

Keep a Value-Behavior Log for the next two weeks, listing how many times you carry out the value-laden actions you described in your second column. Each day, write the heading "Today I acted on my deeper values by:" and then list the behaviors underneath.

For Debbie, the Value-Behavior Exercise and the Value-Behavior Log began the long and difficult healing process, as it has for most of my betrayed clients. Hopefully, it will be the start of healing for you. There will be plenty of additional help throughout the book to regulate high emotional reactivity. At this point, just know that the defensive, reactive you is not the real you, any more than the runny-nose you when you have the flu is the real you. As you begin to heal and grow, defensiveness, high emotional reactivity, resentment, and anger will fade away, and with them, the footprints that betrayal has left on your heart and soul.

Believe it or not, there is a good side to the unique pain of intimate betrayal, although it is hidden in the sometimes obscure message of pain, as we'll see in the next chapter.

Summary

Intimate betrayal is a unique kind of pain with deep biological roots that make its experience seem chaotic, if not a matter of life and death, for most people. Recovery is complicated by natural defenses that inadvertently keep us focused on our injuries and thus embed the footprints of betrayal in the heart and soul. High emotional reactivity creates storms of negative emotions that make it hard to reclaim the true self. High emotional reactivity and the damage it causes will be greatly reduced as we allow ourselves to be guided by deeper values more than temporary feelings.

CHAPTER 2

How to Use the Natural Motivation of Pain to Heal

Pain is a gift. A pain-free life, were it possible, would be numb and short.

The gift of pain lies in its biological function as a dual alarm and motivational system. It dominates attention for one purpose: to motivate behavior that will heal, repair, and improve.

The alarm function of pain is clear—it hurts so much that it is difficult to think about anything else. Its motivational role, though less obvious, is just as compelling. The throbbing in your foot gets you to move the refrigerator off it. An ache in your back gets you to stand up straight and lessen the pressure on your spine. Intestinal pain makes you rock in your chair or get up and move around, to dislodge gas bubbles trapped somewhere in your digestive tract. There is only one place in the body that lacks the nerve endings that originate pain; that is the brain, the one place where corrective behavior is impossible. Injuries to the brain are so often fatal that the need for pain to motivate corrective behavior is nil. (You can remove the arrow from your leg but not from your head.) Except for a sharp sensation in the scalp, injuries to the brain are painless.

The opposite of pain is not pleasure or joy, as popular songs occasionally suggest. The opposite of pain is numbness. For example, suppose you could not remove the refrigerator from your foot and had to wait for help to come. The pain would spike—get worse and worse—up to a point. And then your foot would go numb. Once your brain figures out that no behavior will help, it stops processing the signals of pain from the affected area.

"Where there's pain, there's life," is a saying attributed to the Inuit tribes of Alaska. It literally means that limbs numbed by cold hurt like hell as they return to normal body temperature. If they do not hurt, they are frostbitten—dead—and will need to be removed.

Memories of pain, like the actual experience of it, are utterly necessary for survival and well-being. Recalling that you once burned your finger on a stove makes you more careful when you feel the heat. Remembering that you stepped on a nail last week makes you look before you leap today. Recalling intimate betrayal makes you more cautious about love in the future.

Here's a crucial fact often ignored by some therapists and self-help books: Memories of pain are not about the past; they evolved to keep us safe in the present and future. They point to solutions now, not in the past.

Emotional Pain

Emotional pain serves the same positive function as its physical counterpart. Feeling disregarded, guilty, devalued, or unlovable prompts you to raise self-regard, compensate for any bad behavior, increase your competence, and be more loving. If you do those things, or merely think about doing them, the pain subsides. If you don't, it gets worse and worse until it goes numb. I'm not saying that you have to increase loving behavior toward the partner who betrayed you; that would be too risky in the early part of your recovery. To relieve the pain of feeling unlovable, try to be more loving toward your children or parents or friends, or anyone whom you can love with minimal risk.

If you want to exploit the motivational advantage of emotional pain, you cannot view painful memories as punishments inflicted by others or as self-punishments for past mistakes. They are not punishments to be avoided; they are motivations to heal, improve, repair, and grow.

The Motivational Message of Emotional Pain

Emotional pain takes many forms. Most involve some measure of guilt, anxiety, sorrow, or shame, all of which are abundant after intimate betrayal. Each carries a distinct motivational message of healing.

Guilt comes from a perception that you have violated your values. Although memories of guilt seem to be about the past, their motivational function is to get you to act according to your values *now*, and that is the only thing that will relieve the pain. (More on that in Chapter 8.) Anxiety is dread that something bad will happen; the motivation is to learn more about what might actually happen and develop plans to prevent it, or to cope with it, should it occur. Nothing else will relieve it, although many behaviors—most of them undesirable if not self-destructive—will temporarily avoid it. (More on that in Chapter 11.) Sorrow is about loss of something or someone you value; the message is to invest value in someone else. (This investment is apparent at funerals, where people typically allay their grief by connecting with fellow grievers.) Unless you've been physically traumatized, grief makes you want to hug someone who seems dear to you at the moment. Shame is about failure and inadequacy; the motivation

21

is to reevaluate, reconceptualize, and redouble your efforts to pursue success in love, relationships, or work, or in whatever area you have perceived failure. The experience of shame in and of itself never means that you're a failure; it tells you to stop doing or thinking what you had been thinking or doing and try something different that is consistent with your deeper values. If we follow the motivation of shame—instead of short-circuiting it with resentment, anger, alcohol, workaholism, or whatever—it will lead to healing, improvement, and, ultimately, a solid sense of core value.

How Pain Becomes Suffering

The motivational element of painful emotions has self-healing and self-correcting components. When we take advantage of them, we flourish. When we don't, we suffer. (You've probably heard the saying "Pain is inevitable; suffering is an option.")

If we do not act on its motivation to heal, repair, and improve, the alarm of pain intensifies and generalizes. Just as the untreated toothache becomes facial pain and the neglected foot injury seems to throb along the whole side of the body, unheeded guilt, shame, and anxiety become a generalized kind of "self-ache," which stimulates elaborate defenses that usually include high emotional reactivity, chronic resentment, and frequent anger.

Over time, generalized pain becomes suffering, which results from repeated failure to act on the natural motivation of pain to do something that will heal, repair, or improve. Anything that numbs or avoids pain undermines its function to motivate corrective behavior, and thereby causes suffering. Blame, resentment (expecting someone else to relieve the pain), anger, addictions, and compulsive behavior all render us powerless to heal, improve, or repair. All cause suffering.

Self-compassion vs. self-criticism and self-pity. Self-compassion is a sympathetic response to your hurt, distress, or vulnerability, with a motivation to heal, repair, and improve. It brings a sense of empowerment—a feeling that you can do something to make your life better, even if you are not sure what that might be at the moment. It tends to keep you focused on solutions in the present and future.

Self-criticism is blaming yourself for your hurt, distress, or vulnerability, usually with a measure of punishment or contempt. It's based on the mistaken idea that if you punish yourself enough you won't make similar mistakes in the future, when just the opposite is true—self-punishment leads to more mistakes. (Who is more likely to make more mistakes, the valued self or the devalued self?) Self-pity is focus on your pain or damage with no motivation to heal, repair, or improve. It has an element of contempt for your perceived incompetence or inadequacy because it assumes that you can't do anything to make your life better. Needless to say, self-criticism and self-pity turn pain into suffering.

I'll talk more about self-compassion as the book progresses.

Replace "Why" with "How"

To take advantage of the self-healing and self-correcting features of pain, avoid dwelling on its possible causes. Such ruminations are likely to exacerbate it, for reasons that have nothing to do with the pain. (Mental focus on anything amplifies and magnifies the object of the focus.) Amplifying pain puts too much attention on its alarm component and too little on its motivational element. It's like reacting to the piercing noise of the smoke alarm rather than putting out the fire.

A more important reason to focus on healing and improvement rather than causes is another fact about emotional pain that is often ignored in self-help books: The causes of injury-related pain are not what sustain it. For instance, a piece of broken glass may have sliced your skin open, but the severed and inflamed nerve endings in the flesh sustain the pain. Preoccupation with why you cut yourself will not help to heal the wound. Similarly, your partner lying to you, cheating on you, or abusing you caused your pain. Preoccupation with why he did it runs the risk of making you live inside his head at the cost of your own healing and growth. The pain is telling you to restore self-value now, through your own positive actions, and that is the only thing that will eliminate it.

When clients are referred to me because they've gotten stuck in the thorny aftermath of intimate betrayal, they are invariably preoccupied with why their partners did it to them—or worse, what they might have done to make their partners betray them. That breaks my heart. Not only does focus on the betrayer's motivations distract from healing but speculation about a partner's motives is utterly fruitless. We can never know why someone betrays an intimate bond.

For example, suppose you decide, as most of my clients do at some point, that your partner lied, cheated, or abused you because she was depressed, anxious, deluded, or stressed out, or because she drank too much, exercised too little, or experienced any of a multitude of possible contributing factors. The fact is, most people with those experiences do not betray their loved ones. At best, speculation about your partner's motives may yield possible preconditions for the betrayal, but you'll never accurately identify why your partner chose to betray you.

Rather than speculating about what might have caused your partner to inflict this pain, it is far more to your benefit to concentrate your attention on the internal message of the pain, which is to heal, repair, and improve. The following exercise will help develop the habit of following the deeper message of your pain.

EXERCISE: Find the Healing Message in Your Pain

In one sentence, on a piece of paper, describe some aspect of the pain caused by your partner's betrayal. (Example: "My ex told lies about me to our mutual friends; I feel wronged, angry, and, on a deeper level, unlovable.") Underneath that, answer this question: What is your pain telling you to do now and in the future to heal, repair, and improve? (Example: "It's telling me to improve my relationships with our mutual friends, to be compassionate and not hold their natural feelings of divided loyalty against them. My actions will allow the truth to emerge. Improved connections will heal the sense of isolation caused by the betrayal.")

Hopefully you noticed, in filling out the above exercise, that answering questions about improvement and repair empowers, while focusing on how bad the situation is disempowers. The latter forces the brain to find more and more evidence to support the perception of damage, to prove how bad it is. The former keeps the focus on what you can do to make things better. You may have noticed as well that following the message of your pain leads to your deeper values.

Read your answers to the above aloud right now, and you should notice that your voice strengthens and your posture straightens. That is the usual result of choosing to focus on improvement and repair, even at the very beginning of the healing process.

The following exercise highlights the fact that suffering is prolonged by the meaning we give to our pain. If pain means that we're inadequate, unlovable, or powerless, it turns to suffering. If it means that we're resilient, compassionate, and empowered, we automatically begin the healing process.

EXERCISE: Find the Meaning of Your Pain

In one sentence, on a piece of paper, explain why you are hurt. (Example: "My spouse cheated on me.") Underneath that, answer this question: What does my pain mean about me? First, answer with a negative meaning. (Example: "I'm gullible, a fool, too trusting, all alone and isolated, inadequate, a failure as a partner, unlovable.")

Then answer with a positive meaning. (Example: "I'm resilient, resourceful, human, sensitive, compassionate, empowered.")

Last, write your answer to this question: How can I change a negative meaning to a positive one? (Example: "I can recognize that I have the strength, resilience, and self-compassion to heal this hurt over time. I will stay true to my deepest values; I feel stronger when I do. I will reach out to friends and loved ones and appreciate the world around me. I will recognize human frailty—in myself and in people I care about. I will evaluate my options and choose actions that will lead to a better future.")

The above exercise highlights the fact that suffering results from the meaning we give to our pain. We cannot control what other people do, but we have absolute control over what their behavior means to us. Part II of the book will offer general tools to construct the most beneficial meaning of your experience, to help regulate painful emotions. Return to this exercise once you finish the book, and you should find it much easier to answer the last question.

Effort to Improve

Negative emotions hurt until we start on the path of healing and improving. For example, if you feel a sense of loss, that feeling will tend to worsen, until you begin to think of what you can do to deepen connections with other people in your life. If you feel empty, as many of my betrayed clients report, you don't have to "fill yourself up" to feel better; you just have to try to make your other relationships a little better. The initial motivation of the sense of loss is to get you moving toward something that will reduce the stimulus of the discomfort—in other words, make things a little better. Once you start thinking of what would make things better, the bad feeling begins to subside, freeing up more mental resources in the prefrontal cortex—the problem-solving part of the brain that gets less blood during emotional arousal. With more mental resources applied, success is more likely.

Of course, it would be great if your efforts were successful (for example, if the other parties accepted your attempts to connect). But much of that is out of your control. In the long run, well-being is a function of individual effort more than cooperative success. (Except for brief narcissistic aggrandizement, success in love or work without effort is unsatisfying.) Research shows that what we tend to regret the most is not failure but making insufficient effort (Morrison and Roese 2011).

The rest of the book will guide you through specific ways to heal, repair, and improve.

Summary

Pain is an action signal, a crucial part of the mammalian motivational system that evolved to keep us safe and well. It tells us to do something now that will heal, repair, and improve. That which causes injury-related pain is not the same thing that sustains it. Thus focus on causes of pain tends to worsen and prolong it. Focus on what you can do to improve, even a little, will make the pain subside. Repeated attempts to improve will eventually end the pain. Understanding the message of your pain and controlling the meaning you give to it are necessary steps to keeping safe and well in the future.

CHAPTER 3

How to Develop a Healing Identity

Two points about healing have become clear to me after thousands of hours of work with people who have suffered both common and unimaginable emotional pain. The first is that human beings have an extraordinary capacity for healing emotional wounds. The second truth is this: The most important element in overcoming emotional pain is developing a *healing identity*.

With a healing identity, you will identify with your strengths, resilience, and desire to improve your life. Your decision to develop a healing identity will free you from the debilitating thoughts of damage, unfairness, and blame that inevitably occur after intimate betrayal. You will continue to have such thoughts for a time, and occasionally feel overwhelmed by them. But for the most part, a healing identity will help you resist the impulse to focus on them, thus amplifying and magnifying them. Instead, a healing identity makes you look for opportunities to heal, improve, and grow.

Why Identity Is Important

A brief description of the form and function of identity will show why a healing identity is so important in recovery from intimate betrayal. Identity has an internal component (how we're inclined to see ourselves) and a social component (how we want others to see us). It's composed of:

- perceived or desired personal qualities (such as intelligence, stupidity, compassion, resilience, strength, weakness, or rebelliousness)

- characteristic behaviors (such as helping, teaching, listening, encouraging, or criticizing)

- social roles (such as parent, writer, good friend, moral person, winner, doormat, or victim)

Identity exerts far-reaching influence on our thoughts, feelings, and behavior, due to its function as an organizer of experience and a filter of information the brain selects to process. Left on automatic pilot, our brains look for information conforming to identity and overlook disconfirming evidence. The psychological advantage is this: if consistent and (more or less) accurate, identity reduces self-doubt and indecisiveness by presenting a clear repertoire of thoughts and behavior.

For example, if I identify with being a teacher, I will know what to think and do in the classroom. I'll focus on ways to help my students grasp complicated material, taking into account their particular learning needs. (Though if I identify just with being knowledgeable, I'll be preoccupied with showing off what I know, and perhaps even regard my students' confusion as an indication of how much smarter I am.) If I'm unsure of my identity, I will likely bumble along with a soulless, "textbook" kind of teaching, and will likely be as unsatisfied with my work as I am unfair to my students.

You Don't Deserve to Suffer from Victim Identity

Absent the conscious choice to develop a healing identity, intimate betrayal can easily lead to *victim identity*—identification with hurt and bad treatment. Damage, injury, defects, and weakness become integral aspects of the identity that is likely to emerge after intimate betrayal.

Victim identity has dire implications for recovery (beyond the fact that it's difficult to marshal mental resources for healing when focused on perceived damage and weakness). It can give this completely false impression: If you didn't have your pain or bear the scars of mistreatment, you wouldn't know who you are. I've had so many clients begin therapy with an unspoken self-doubt. If they had the words, it would sound like this: "Who am I, if not an abused woman?" (or a "cuckolded husband," or a "doormat," or a "sap who married a thief.")

In advanced forms of victim identity, the motivation of pain to heal, improve, and grow is completely lost. Instead, pain becomes a monument similar to ruins preserved after a war to serve as a perpetual reminder of the suffering it caused. For example, Sarah first came to treatment with a confession: For a long time, she didn't want to relieve her anxiety, depression, and insomnia, because that would let her cheating husband "off the hook."

"He has to see what he's done to me," she declared. "He has to take responsibility for how much of a shit he is. He has to admit that I didn't deserve to be harmed like this. He should feel horrible for what he's done to me."

Sarah's husband had stonewalled her completely after she discovered his affairs, giving her the understandable impression that he didn't care how hurt she was. In truth, he couldn't bear to see what he had done to her. Stonewalling, though shameful, is an attempt to avoid shame (Gottman et al. 1994; Love and Stosny 2008). When he could no longer avoid the pain he had caused her, when he realized how thin, wan, and exhausted she had grown, he dropped into an abyss of shame. Unable to face her, he moved out of the house in the middle of the night, leaving a note that read "I will never forgive myself for the irreparable damage I have done to you. You were too good of a person for me, and I ruined you. I failed unforgivably. I can't let myself bring you down anymore through my presence in your life. You deserve so much better."

Although she would have preferred to hear it from her husband in person, Sarah got the admission she had wanted from the moment she discovered his affairs. He validated her pain. He validated the way she saw herself—as damaged. He hated himself for doing it to her. He said all that she thought she wanted to hear. Yet getting what she thought she wanted made her more depressed than ever.

"I don't really miss him," she told me. "I knew our marriage was over long ago. But I thought that once he acknowledged the damage he'd done to me I would feel better. Now I just feel numb and hopeless."

Sarah's successful treatment began, as it does for all my clients, with a commitment to a healing identity, which helped her focus on her strengths and resilience. Although her relationship with her ex-husband was damaged beyond repair, *she* was not damaged in any way—not as a person, parent, friend, or employee. Her personal qualities, her values, her spirit, and all her talents and abilities were intact, requiring only her attention to flourish.

The same is true of you. You are not damaged. Your personal qualities, values, spirit, talents, and abilities are intact, requiring only your attention to bloom. The exercise below will start you on the path to a solid healing identity.

EXERCISE: Create a Healing Identity

Step One: Inventory

On a piece of paper, list your strengths (for example: intelligence, curiosity, resourcefulness, creativity, adaptability, courage, sense of humor, persistence, curiosity, open-mindedness, integrity, bravery, vitality, humility).

List your deeper values (for example: honesty, responsibility, appreciation of nature and creative beauty, spirituality, compassion, sense of community, fairness, gratitude, ability to love).

List evidence of your resilience (for example: how you recovered from past illnesses, loss, setbacks, failures, or grief).

Write what you would say to close friends who listed all the strengths, values, and resilience you have listed but, due to their hurt, were self-critical and prone to underestimate their self-value.

Step Two: Commitment

Explain how you will employ your strengths and use your deeper values for healing. (Example: I will investigate opportunities for growth in work and social life, make it a point to see the perspectives of my friends and loved ones alongside my own, focus on those aspects of life that broaden my perspective, and allow myself to appreciate beauty in nature and in creative endeavors.)

Step Three: Declaration

Write the following declaration, and sign it: I hereby resolve to focus my attention and behavior on what will help me heal, grow, improve, and create value in my life.

Step Four: Opportunities for Growth

Make a list of the opportunities for growth that are presented by the pain you have suffered. (Example: I will have a deeper knowledge of myself and others. I will have a deeper appreciation of those who struggle to grow from the ruins of life's setbacks and misfortunes. I will resurrect my abandoned dreams by taking courses, looking up old friends, starting a small business, and doing volunteer work in my community.)

Step Five: Spiritual Testament

Write the following declaration, and sign it: "I will transcend all that I have suffered and come out of this recovery period a better person, focused on a permanent sense of meaning and purpose, according to the spiritual beliefs that resonate in my soul."

Now read the declaration out loud. (We tend to be more committed to statements we write down and say out loud than to those we merely think to ourselves.) You should feel empowered as you read. If not, circle the part where your sense of empowerment fades. Return to the exercise after you complete Part II, when you'll have more tools for self-empowerment.

Stay True to Yourself

Intimate betrayal carries a natural impulse to retaliate. Some part of you wants to hurt your betrayer at least as much as you've been hurt. Don't get me wrong; your partner may well deserve to be hurt. But that's not the point. More important than what your partner might deserve is the fact that you do not deserve to suffer the entirely negative and no-win consequences of victim identity.

Many of my clients admit that what most prompted them to seek treatment was that they didn't like the person they'd become. The retaliation reflex tends to extend beyond the offending partner, as it burrows into the core of your defensive system. In other words, intimate betrayal creates an impulse to devalue everyone who invokes negative feelings. You may have noticed since the betrayal that you've had frequent impulses to be more critical, blaming, and controlling in your dealings with other people. Yet you know in your heart that acting on these impulses would violate your deeper values. Acting on them repeatedly would alienate you from your core self and turn you into someone you are not. Ironically, acting on the impulse to retaliate would make you less like yourself and more like your betrayer. It would embed the footprints of betrayal in your heart and soul.

Severe emotional injury of any kind, including intimate betrayal, can work like the bite of the vampire. Once bitten, we have an impulse to bite others. Examples of the most extreme cases of this phenomenon are seen in domestic violence offenders and other violent criminals, who almost invariably suffer from victim identity. In their minds, the hurt they have suffered in the past justifies their crimes and abuse in the present (Katz 1990; Rhodes 1999; Stosny 1995).

There is only one kind of retaliation that assures escape from the pitfalls of victim identity. As expressed in the old saying, "the greatest revenge is living well." After intimate betrayal, "living well" means healing, growing, and creating a value-filled life.

If you feel that you've lost yourself since the betrayal, know that it is only a temporary condition. Your healing identity will get you back to the person you really are and help you stay true to yourself. Never react in kind to your betrayer's unconscionable behavior or become the kind of person your betraying partner deserves. Be the person you truly are, committed to healing, improving, and growth.

You're Different from Your Betrayer

During your recovery, it's vital to keep in mind how different you are from your betrayer and how you would have behaved differently in his shoes. Keeping a behavioral log each day for the next few weeks will etch the differences in your mind. Feel the power in the differences as you write.

BEHAVIORAL LOG

On a piece of paper or a calendar, write the headings "What my partner did:" and "What I do:" for each day for the next two to four weeks. On each of those days, you will record the differences you observe between the behavior of your betrayer and your own behavior. (The point of the repetition is to help you internalize the differences between you and your partner, while, at the same time, fortifying your deeper values.) Draw from any of the following examples that apply to your relationship.

What my partner did:

My partner lied to me.

What I do:

Today I was truthful in all my relationships.

What my partner did:

My partner cheated on me.

What I do:

Today I was loyal and sensitive to the well-being of those I love.

What my partner did:

My partner stole from me.

What I do:

Today I was honest and fair in all my relationships.

What my partner did:

My partner abused me.

What I do:

Today I was compassionate to those I love.

What my partner did:

My partner was selfish throughout our relationship.

What I do:

Today I was sensitive to the well-being of those I love.

What my partner did:

My partner was manipulative of our friends.

What I do:

Today I was supportive of my friends.

What my partner did:

My partner was mean to our pets.

What I do:

Today I was kind to our pets.

What my partner did:

My partner made fun of me for reading.

What I do:

Today I enjoyed learning.

Keeping this log for a few weeks will strengthen your healing identity by shifting focus from the bad things your partner did to the good things that you do.

Healing vs. Retaliation

The impulse to retaliate—and thereby act like your betrayer—will do no harm if it is regulated and channeled into more beneficial behavior. Below is an exercise you can do to help gauge progress in maintaining your healing identity. Don't worry if you don't manage to regulate all your impulses at the time they occur; it's unlikely that you'll be able to do so at this early stage of recovery. Just fill in what you intend to do in the future.

REGULATING THE IMPULSE TO RETALIATE

Create a weekly log to track your impulses and how you regulate them. Each week, record whether and how often you felt the impulse to criticize, act superior, devalue or demean, or inflict emotional or physical harm. Then explain how you focused on what would help you heal, repair, and improve. Examples follow.

This week I felt the impulse to criticize several times.

How I regulated the impulse: I reminded myself of what is really important to me—namely, making my behavior consistent with my deeper values.

This week, at least once, I felt the impulse to act superior.

How I regulated the impulse: I focused on improving myself by eating healthfully, resting, and exercising.

This week, a few times, I felt the impulse to devalue or demean.

How I regulated the impulse: I reminded myself of my deeper values of equality and respect.

This week (more times than I can count), I felt the impulse to inflict emotional or physical harm.

How I regulated the impulse: I allowed myself to fantasize a little about revenge, but reminded myself that what is more important to me is making my behavior consistent with my deeper values.

The above exercise is intended to show that remaining true to your deeper values provides more empowerment for a longer period of time than indulging in retaliation impulses. That's because you are probably not a vindictive person, so acting on retaliation impulses violates your deeper sense of self. Revenge, when it violates your deeper values, is sweet only for a very, very short time.

Healing Identity vs. Blame

The fact that you have suffered intimate betrayal gives you every right to blame your injuries on your betrayer; of course he is to blame for your hurt. However, there's a problem with blame while recovering from intimate betrayal: it renders you completely powerless over your emotional well-being.

I once had a bright and beautiful client whose husband of five years had been unfaithful to her. When I first met Cindy, she described her husband's efforts to make amends as "nothing short of heroic."

"He does everything right," she said with palpable embarrassment, as if it were her fault that her wounds had not healed. His remorse and his attempts at loving behavior only made her feel more ashamed. "That's a kick, isn't it? He has an affair, and I feel guilty! And then I think, if he hadn't done that, I wouldn't be sitting here now, damaged."

Cindy's husband was clearly to blame for her pain. But he could not heal it, despite his apparent efforts to repair their relationship and his strong desire to help her recover. The root of her pain—what hurt the most—was that his behavior made her feel unlovable. As much as he wanted to do more, the best that he could do was make her feel loved. Unfortunately, that would not be enough, as long as she felt unlovable.

Feeling worthy of love rises ultimately from our own behavior; to feel lovable, you have to be loving. While it is easier to feel lovable—in other words, to behave in loving ways—when we feel loved, being loved is simply not enough to make us feel lovable. When we don't feel worthy of love, being loved, while perhaps flattering, makes us feel like we're getting something we don't deserve. In the long run it makes us feel inadequate, to the extent that we can't quite muster the emotional reserves to return the love we're getting. People who don't feel lovable cannot receive love for very long.

Cindy had to replace her false sense of being damaged (and the blame it engendered) with a healing identity, which would restore the truth about her. She was abundantly worthy of love but not because her husband loved her. She was lovable because she loved, cared for, and felt compassion for the significant people in her life. Developing a healing identity shifted her focus onto what she could do to feel lovable, naturally leading to healing and growth. (We'll return later in the book to Cindy's happy outcome, which began the day she committed to a healing identity.)

A Healing Identity Is Responsible and Powerful

It may seem patently unfair that the injured party in an intimate betrayal has to take responsibility for her personal healing. That's because healing has nothing to do with fairness; it has to do with power. Where blame renders us powerless, responsibility empowers us.

For example, it was clearly unfair that I was mugged while walking down the street one night. But while my assailant was entirely to blame for the crime, I was entirely responsible for healing my wounds. I could get away with blaming him for my physical injuries, as I must confess I did for a day or so. My physical injuries would heal on their own, albeit with less efficiency had I continued to indulge my feelings of powerlessness and anger. (Anger suppresses the immune system, Williams and Williams 1993.) However, my psychological wounds never would have healed so long as I stayed focused on the terrible behavior of my assailant. Not until I accepted responsibility to heal myself could I focus my mental resources on what I could do to feel whole and valuable again. Only then did I gain power over my emotional well-being. I developed a healing identity that marshaled my mental, emotional, and spiritual resources for healing, improvement, and growth.

HEALING IDENTITY EXERCISE

This exercise will help you appreciate the contrasting effects of blame and a healing identity.

> Take a moment to think about your most recent bad mood. List three things that might have caused it (for example: thinking about the betrayal, trouble with family members or friends, and friction at work).
>
> Indicate who is to blame for each item you listed above. If the blame is egregious, write "a lot" next to the name.
>
> Now take three minutes to write down what you can do to improve the things that triggered your bad mood. Time yourself. Stop writing after three minutes, whether you have come up with something or not.

Invoke Your Healing Identity

> List your strengths (for example: intelligence, curiosity, resourcefulness, creativity, adaptability, courage, sense of humor, persistence, curiosity, open-mindedness, integrity, bravery, vitality, humility, humor).
>
> List your deeper values (for example: honesty, responsibility, appreciation of nature and creative beauty, spirituality, compassion, sense of community, fairness, gratitude, ability to love).
>
> List evidence of your resilience (for example, how you recovered from past illnesses, loss, setbacks, failures, or grief).

Once again take three minutes to think of what you can do to improve the things that triggered the bad mood you described above. Time yourself. Stop after three minutes, whether you have come up with something or not.

As you completed the exercise, you probably noticed that thoughts of improvement came more easily when you abandoned blame in favor of a healing identity.

Keeping a daily log will reinforce your healing identity. Each powerless thought and destructive impulse must be associated with a desirable answer in your head. Repetition of the association conditions, or trains, the brain to veer into more constructive thoughts, feelings, and behavior whenever the undesirable ones occur.

To create a Daily Healing Identity Log, each day record your blaming thoughts. (Example: My partner ruined my life, disrupted the lives of our children, caused needless harm, and created financial hardship.) Next, add your retaliation impulses. (Example: I wanted to curse my ex, tell my children how bad their mother really is, report her to the IRS, slash her tires, throw eggs at her house, and cause her serious harm.)

Then, write down your "healing identity response." (Example: Thinking and acting this way will not help me heal, improve, and grow. Instead, I will focus on how resilient I am. I will help my children appreciate all that is good in their lives, and help them realize their enormous potential to grow and learn. I will pray for all those who have lost their way, do something kind for myself and a friend, exercise regularly, take care of my health, and focus on how to make the best of my life. I will heal my hurt and work to the best of my ability to overcome financial hardship by detailed planning and whatever else it takes.)

Fill out the log every day for the next three to six weeks, or until the healing identity responses seem automatic to you.

Hopefully you now feel committed to a healing identity, which will marshal your mental resources for healing and growth. The next chapter describes the mechanisms of emotional healing and offers tools to facilitate the remarkable human ability to heal and grow.

Summary

If we do not make the conscious choice to forge a healing identity—by focusing on strengths, resilience, and deeper values—most of us, by default, develop victim identity—a focus on hurt and mistreatment, and a perception of being damaged and weakened. The decision to identify with your capacity to heal and grow marshals your intellectual, emotional, and spiritual resources toward healing the hurt of intimate betrayal and outgrowing its otherwise indelible scars.

CHAPTER 4

How to Use Restorative Images to Heal Painful Memories

Neuroscience has revealed something all too familiar to those who have lived through intimate betrayal: emotional pain is just as real to the brain as physical pain (McDonald and Leary 2005). Now here's the good news: emotional healing is just as real to the brain as physical healing.

Physiological healing is the revitalization of diseased or injured tissue, organs, or biological systems. Simply put, the body's cells regenerate or repair to reduce the size of the distressed or damaged area and restore the body to normal functioning.

Emotional healing is more complicated and less mechanistic, but otherwise follows a similar path to restoration. It can be accomplished with as much efficiency and effectiveness as the wondrous healing of our bodies.

Emotional healing happens when the brain replaces painful memories (images) of injury or damage with *restorative images*, which motivate behavior that promotes safety, growth, and well-being, thereby restoring the normal function of the mind. The process occurs naturally for most people, although it takes a long while.

Recovery from common grief over the death of a loved one is the paradigm of how the mind heals itself. In the beginning of the grief process, memories of the deceased amplify the sense of loss and inhibit premature emotional investment in others. For a while, the pain is acute. Yet over time, the mind focuses less and less on what has been lost. This mental shift of focus away from loss allows positive experiences with the deceased—restorative images—to dominate memory. It becomes pleasant to think about the lost loved one. At that point, emotional healing has occurred.

I was quite aware of these facts about recovery from grief after more than a decade of research and clinical observations. But my intellectual understanding held no emotional significance beyond empathy for others—until my mother died.

The sudden and completely unexpected death of my mother turned my world upside down. In the weeks and months after her death it hurt so much to think of her that I avoided all conscious reminders of her. Photos were packed away; her favorite things were stored; her music was silenced.

I should have known that such a strategy was doomed to failure. Consciousness can be stubborn, but it is subject to exhaustion, while the unconscious, where hidden memories dominate, persists even in sleep and dreams. A few months after her death, I woke up in the middle of the night and groped for a piece of paper and pen to write down something that seemed terribly important in that half-dream state. Although my pen had perforated the paper by pressing it against the soft bed, I could make out what I'd scribbled by the light of morning: "The most important thing in my life is the death of my mother."

Despite my considerable clinical experience at the time, I had not noticed how depressed I'd become during those months. But my dark mood began to lift that morning, when I realized that the sentence I had written on that small, perforated piece of paper the night before was completely false. The most important thing in my life was not the death of my mother. Far more important was her life.

When we lose loved ones, we lose nothing we ever experienced with them. All that I lost of my mother was the future with her, which I never actually had. I began to focus on memories of the many positive experiences I had with her—experiences that I would never lose.

At last my professional training in behavioral conditioning (forging mental, emotional, and behavior associations through repetition) became useful. I recalled many images of my mother that embodied love, wisdom, support, and enjoyment. I associated those with each painful memory that came to me. I repeated the association of hurtful images with restorative ones over and over, conditioning the painful memories to stimulate the occurrence of restorative images automatically.

After a few weeks it became pleasurable and rewarding to think about my mother. Now, when my mood is down for any reason, I try to think of her, and, invariably, I find my way out of the doldrums.

I'm quite sure that I did not create a healing process to overcome the grief caused by my mother's death. All I did was inadvertently hasten the brain's natural process of healing emotional pain through intentional reconditioning of painful memories.

Recovery from intimate betrayal is more complicated than simple grief. Yet the same process of conditioning restorative images to heal memories of pain has worked for thousands of my clients who have suffered one or more forms of intimate betrayal.

Restorative Images

A restorative image is any emotionally laden bit of your imagination that eases pain by shifting mental focus from loss to growth. The most potent images are usually drawn from experience—something you've seen, heard, smelled, touched, or dreamed. The images can be beautiful, meaningful, exciting, stunning, soothing, or peaceful. They can also be purely made-up—one of mine is moving rapidly through an expanding portion of deep space ablaze with the light of billions of stars. Restorative images remind us that our sense of who we are rises from what we have gained in life, rather than what we've lost or suffered, and is continually strengthened by our ability to improve and grow. The most powerful restorative images are those that reinforce our deepest values. Anthropological evidence suggests that certain categories of values have existed to some extent since the earliest emergence of the human species and are fertile ground for restorative images. They are:

- basic humanity (innate capacity for interest in the well-being of others)

- love

- spiritual connection

- appreciation of natural and creative beauty

- community connection (identifying with, or feeling connected to, a group of people)

- compassionate behavior (crucial to the maintenance of social bonds)

Emotional healing is largely a process of calling up images that reinforce these deep values, and reconditioning your brain to associate them with painful memories.

Recondition Your Brain

Brain conditioning is a process of repeating tasks or mental associations until new habits in sequences of neural firing are formed. When it comes to emotions, we are almost entirely creatures of habit. By the time we're adults, the vast majority of our emotions are conditioned by past experiences. In other words, when a certain kind of thing happens, we have a certain *habituated* emotional response. The brain develops so many conditioned responses because they are metabolically cheap; they consume little energy compared to conscious intentions. (The difference in mental exertion between a habituated response and a consciously decided action is hundreds of millions of multifiring neurons.) We're reconditioning our brains all the time, usually in adaptation to our environments. Now is the time to take up the process consciously in the service of healing and growth.

Because habituated responses get repeated thousands of times over the years, there is only one way the brain can form new habits, and that is through repetition of new associations. Specifically, we must practice associating restorative images with memories of pain. But don't worry; it won't take nearly as many repetitions to undo the habit as it took to form it in the first place. Restorative images have a potent reinforcement because they make you feel better. In general, it takes less iteration for a more pleasant habit to replace a painful one.

Practice, Practice, Practice

To get the most out of the exercise that follows, make a list of your more prominent painful memories. Practice associating at least one of your restorative images with each item, every day, until the new associations become automatic. Habit formation should occur within six weeks of practice. Then, each time a painful image occurs in implicit or unconscious memory, its restorative counterpart will occur almost simultaneously. Painful memories will indirectly stimulate the restorative images and motivate behavior that promotes healing and growth.

RESTORATIVE IMAGE EXERCISE

Describe your emotional hurt. (Example: My ex, in a drunken rage, hit me repeatedly with a stick. I can feel the throbbing deep in the bones of my arms where the stick landed, as I tried to cover my head. Everything hurts. I'm so ashamed.)

Choose an image of basic humanity that is meaningful to you. *(Example: Rescuing a child in danger—from an auto crash, fire, drowning, or some other tragic circumstance—is one of the most powerful of healing images. It dislodges the self-obsession of pain and activates a sense of humanity. To heal is to feel more humane.)*

Associate the image with your painful memory. *(Example: I crawl away from the beating I experienced to help this desperate child, who is alone and terrified. I comfort her, as she clings to me, feeling my protection. My pain fades as I hold her, feeling her head on my chest, her heart beating with mine. I outgrow the pain.)*

Choose an image of love that is meaningful to you *(something you associate with love, such as a picture, a scent, or the touch of a loved one).*

Associate the image with your painful memory. *(Example: My daughter as a young child, curled in her blanket, sleeping—next to this loving image, the memory of my beating evaporates.)*

Choose an image of spirituality that is meaningful to you *(something that evokes a sense of connection to something larger than the self—such as God, nature, the cosmos, a social or moral cause, or the sea of humanity).*

Associate the image with your painful memory.
(Example: Standing on a boat at sea, staring at the wide expanse of stars, I feel connected to the universe. This image transcends my painful memory.)

Choose an image of natural or creative beauty that is meaningful to you *(something in nature that moves you or something creative in the form of art, literature, architecture, music, dance, furniture, jewelry, or anything created by another person).*

Associate the image with your painful memory.
(Example: The sun setting over the Grand Canyon helps heal the painful recollection.)

Choose an image of community connection that is meaningful to you *(something that invokes a sense of connection or identification with a group of people).*

Associate the image with your painful memory.
(Example: As a member of my neighborhood-watch committee, I connect with a diverse group of people dedicated to making our neighborhood safe, especially for children. I imagine myself protecting all the people in my neighborhood. This image overwhelms the memory of my pain.)

Choose an image of a small compassionate act that is meaningful to you *(for example, helping someone struggling with packages, talking to someone who is down, or visiting someone who is sick).*

Associate the image with your painful memory.
(Example: Delivering hot dinners to the isolated elderly in a snowstorm is more important to me than the memory of my pain.)

Of course, the first few times you practice associating your restorative images with memories of pain, you will notice, at best, short-lived results. You'll feel better, but only for a while. The connection must be repeated many times to form a conditioned response.

If you notice only a little improvement after a couple of weeks of practice, try going through your list of painful memories up to six or seven times a day. Doing so will *desensitize* them. One of the oldest and most effective behavioral therapy techniques, desensitization reduces the emotional intensity of a behavior or memory by repeating it in safer contexts. Desensitization may well take more repetitions when the painful memories are virulent, but your emotional healing and ultimate well-being are worth the effort.

My client Madeline is an excellent example of the way many people have used desensitization to aid the reconditioning process. Madeline had been divorced from an unfaithful, verbally abusive, and financially domineering man for years when she came to see me. Though only forty-one years old, she had neither desired nor attempted a serious relationship since her divorce. In truth, she had never emotionally left her marriage. Painful memories of its multiple betrayals continued to haunt her and, to a large extent, control her life. When she saw an attractive woman on the street, in a store, or at a party, she was likely to think of her husband flirting with other women (lewdly, by her description), right in front of her. She'd become tense and irritable at the mere sight of a pretty face. Then she would think of times her husband had abused her and lied to her. (Once an emotional state is stimulated, memories of experiences in that same emotional state are more readily accessible. That's how painful memories can seem to cascade like a waterfall once they get started.) The problem was not that Madeline couldn't let go of her marriage; it was that she couldn't dislodge the footprints of intimate betrayal from her heart and soul.

Madeline began the long-overdue healing process with her commitment to a healing identity. She then made a list of all the memories of the multiple betrayals of her marriage that she could conjure. With each item on her rather long list, she associated these restorative images: comforting a frightened child; holding both her children when they were babies; a Christian cross coming out of a bright sky; a choppy ocean smashing against rocks beneath a cliff; her favorite necklace, which was made for her by a close friend; the sense of fellowship she enjoyed at her political action committee meetings; and helping her neighbor, whose arthritis was flaring up, pull weeds from her garden.

Her reconditioning plan began, as it does for most of my clients, with putting aside fifteen to twenty minutes every day to go over her complete list of painful memories, associating each item with her restorative images. After a couple of weeks, the exercise was still very difficult for her. (In most cases it becomes much easier after a few days.) She increased her practice sessions to seven times per day, repeating the associations for as long as it took to feel calm—usually around ten minutes. Within six weeks of practice, she had desensitized her painful memories, while reconditioning them to invoke her restorative images automatically.

She was now willing and eager to build more value and meaning into her life, knowing that doing so is the best way to heal and grow from intimate betrayal. How to build more value and meaning into your life is the theme of the rest of this book.

Summary

Under ordinary circumstances, emotional healing occurs naturally, but over a long period of time. Due to the special complications of intimate betrayal, the healing process can take forever if left to its own devices. But the process can be greatly accelerated by intentionally conditioning restorative images to occur automatically when painful memories occur. This reconditioning process requires frequent practice until new habits are formed.

Continue to practice your reconditioning skills as you begin Part II, which addresses how to retrain the recovering heart.

Part II

Retraining the Recovering Heart

Emotional healing and growth are inherently general processes, even when the injuries that necessitate them have very specific causes. Just as the harm of a gunshot wound threatens the general health of the body, not merely the wounded area, intimate betrayal goes well beyond issues of trust and love to infect the way we make sense of our lives in general. In a very real sense, the meaning of your life changed after the betrayal.

Just as treatment of physical wounds must boost the entire immune system to restore the general health of the body, emotional healing and growth must augment the psychological equivalent of the immune system to restore the general health of the mind, particularly its ability to create a life you fully value, with a palpable sense of meaning and purpose. The key to healing and growth is strengthening what I believe is the immune system of the mind—that which creates a general sense of value, meaning, and purpose in life. I call it *core value*.

CHAPTER 5

The Key to Healing and Growth: Your Core Value

Core value grows out of the uniquely human drive to create value—to make people, things, and ideas important enough to appreciate, nurture, and protect. Consistently acting on the drive to create value provides a sense of meaning and purpose in life. This chapter and the next will help develop your core value as a general means of healing and growth. Although a highly developed core value won't make you forget your betrayal, it will definitely make all that you have suffered less important in your life as a whole. The past can no longer control us, once it is overshadowed by the deeply human drive to create value and give our lives meaning.

The Drive to Create Value

Although we have an innate drive to create value, we have to make choices of who and what to value. A sunset has value if, and only if, you give it value—you invest energy and effort to fully perceive it, thus allowing you to appreciate it. While it does nothing for the sunset if you value it, valuing it does wonders for you. The moment of value creation makes you feel more vital, engaged, interested, appreciative—in short, more alive. Life means more to you at the instant you create value, just as it means less to you when you are not creating value. Most positive emotion, passion, meaning, purpose, and conviction come from creating value, and most emptiness, aggression, and depression result from failure to create value.

Virtually all our accomplishments occur through value creation, and virtually all our failures owe to devaluing (value destruction). Consider who is more likely to maintain healthy weight: the person who values health or the one who devalues her body? Who is more likely to succeed with fewer mistakes, the coach who values the skills and cohesiveness of the team or the one who devalues his players? Who will do better at work and feel more satisfied with it, the employee who values her contribution and her coworkers, or the one who devalues his job, peers, or managers? Now here's the really important question: Who is more likely to thrive after intimate betrayal, the betrayed partner who values her well-being, her other relationships, her strengths, and her resilience, or the one who devalues his life and most of the people in it?

Unfortunately, there's a large problem with core value: Creating value consumes enormous amounts of energy. It takes a lot more effort to appreciate a sunset or a child's smile than to ignore them. Most of us try to conserve our limited stores of energy by withholding the necessary components of value creation: interest and attention. If we withhold too much too often, we'll end up running mostly on automatic pilot, just going through the motions of living. Eventually, we'll get depressed. Depression can be understood as extremely low value creation.

A common way to avoid the depressed mood of low value creation is to devalue—to lower the value of someone or something by deciding that "he's not good enough," or "that's not worth it," or "I'm not worth it." Devaluing brings a temporary spike in energy, because it invokes a subtle form of anger or disgust directed at yourself or others. Devaluing behaviors (such as criticism, verbal aggression, and actions motivated by contempt or disgust) feel briefly more empowering than the depressed mood of low value creation.

Everyone devalues sometimes, and we're especially prone to it after intimate betrayal. But in the long run, if you devalue more than you value, your life will be pretty bad, even if a lot of good things happen to you. I've seen considerable evidence of this since my frequent media appearances have attracted some rich, famous, and powerful clients, whose lives are filled with good fortune. It's amazing how creative they are at finding ways to make themselves miserable, simply because they choose to devalue more than they value.

On the other side of the coin, if you value more than you devalue, your life will be good, even if a lot of bad things happen. My primary example is a mother I knew who lost both her teenage sons. Within a year, one son died in an accident and the other was killed while defending a preteen girl, whom he didn't know, from a bully's unwanted advances. Out of nowhere, this woman's only children were taken from her. Yet she turned the deaths of her sons into inspiration for other members of the community through her impassioned advocacy for various youth groups. She was the most charismatic and genuine person I've ever met, because, despite the enormity of her misfortunes, she valued more than she devalued.

States of Core Value and How to Access Them

Like all psychological drives, core value works as an unconscious component of the human motivational system. However, to aid in healing and growth, it can be cultivated as a conscious mental state, in which you focus your thoughts, emotions, and behaviors on increasing the value of your experience and staying true to what is most important to you. The more you do this, the stronger your core value grows and the less likely you are to feel devalued, inadequate, or unlovable as a result of your partner's (or anyone else's) behavior.

Developing core value as a mental state will provide a place within, where you can go, at any time, under any kind of stress or depressed mood, to revitalize your desire to create value and meaning in your life. It will function as a primary defense against future hurt of any kind (not just intimate betrayal) and offer the greatest potential for personal healing and growth.

There are many paths to a conscious state of core value. Here are three:

1. Honor the most important thing about you as a person.

2. Prove to yourself that you are worthy by doing something that makes you feel lovable and adequate.

3. Act on any one of the *core value motivations*.

Path One: Honor the Most Important Thing about You

Please write down your answer to the following question. (Writing it down invokes a motor skill, which is more likely to embed what you write in implicit memory, increasing the likelihood that you'll automatically assume it the future.)

"What is the most important thing about me as a person?"

I'm guessing that you wrote something like "I'm honest" or "loyal" or "generous" or "a hard worker," because that's how most of my clients initially respond. These are significant qualities, to be sure, but they're not the most important thing about you. (It's a hard question to answer, because we don't typically think about our most essential qualities.) Here's a way to tease out what you might regard as the single most important thing about you:

If you don't have grown children, imagine that you do. Choose how you would rather your grown children—real or imagined—feel about you:

Choice A: "[Mom or Dad] was honest, loyal, generous, and hard-working. I'm not sure [she or he] really cared about me, but [she or he] was always honest, loyal, generous, and hard-working."

Choice B: "[Mom or Dad] was human, and [she or he] made a few mistakes. But there was never any doubt that [she or he] cared about me and wanted what was best for me."

If love is so important to you that intimate betrayal has been devastating, rather than a mere ego offense, its likely that the most important thing about you is your capacity to show care and compassion for the people you love.

If you have a different answer to the "most important thing about you" question, try to take it a step deeper by asking yourself "*Why* is this important to me? Is this what I will be most proud of near the end of my life? Is it what I will most regret not doing enough of?"

Read out loud whatever you wrote down as the most important thing about you. When you do, you will feel either empowered or uneasy. The latter indicates that you need to adjust your behavior to be consistent with your most important quality, to avoid hidden feelings of guilt, shame, anxiety, regret, inadequacy, or unworthiness. There are built-in rewards for staying true to what you regard as the most important thing about you: a sense of authenticity and conviction, with relatively little self-doubt. Those rewards are available in states of core value, which you can invoke most easily by honoring the most important thing about you as a person.

Path Two: Prove to Yourself That You're Worthy

Emotions are sometimes complicated, but in terms of motivation, they're not rocket science. You prove to yourself that you're respectable, valuable, and lovable by respecting, valuing, and loving. There's really no other way to do it. (Other people respecting, valuing, and loving you won't feel genuine if you're not respectful, valuing, and loving.) And if you prove these things to yourself, you won't feel a need to prove them to anyone else. Respectful, valuing, and loving people will recognize these qualities in you. As for those who do not, you can sympathize with their need to heal and grow.

Write the following declaration, and then read it aloud, with all the conviction you can muster. (Once again, we tend to be more committed to statements we write down and say out loud than those we merely think to ourselves.)

"I know that I am worthy of respect, value, and compassion, because I'm respectful to all people, I value many, and I love a few. I feel compassion for the distress and pain of my loved ones and, when possible, try my best to help."

Now, on a piece of paper, describe your declaration in behavioral terms: How will you show respect, value, and compassion for loved ones? (Example: I will talk to them the way that I want them to talk to me. I will let them know that I care about their well-being. I will show that I want to help when they are in pain or distress.)

You will find, as you do the things you wrote down, that a sense of personal power comes from doing what you sincerely believe is the right thing. You will then become less dependent on the response of others, who may not be able to invoke their own core value to validate you. In other words, an unfavorable response from others will be disappointing but will not make you feel unworthy of respect, value, and love. You will need less validation of those qualities from others, because states of core value are self-validating.

Path Three: Act on a Core Value Motivation

A third way to access core value is to act on any one of what I call the *core value motivations:*

- improve

- appreciate

- protect

- connect

If you're in a state of core value, you're automatically trying to do one of the above. Fortunately, core value is a two-way street. When you find yourself cut off from your drive to create value—in other words, you feel numb, down, nervous, resentful, or aggressive—deliberate attempts to improve or appreciate or connect or protect will access a state of core value and set you once again on the road to healing and growth.

Improve. The core value motivation to improve means striving to make something better. For optimal success in recovering from the severe effects intimate betrayal, think of improving as an incremental process—making things a little better at a time. People sometimes stop trying to improve because they don't know how to "fix" a situation. In emotionally charged conditions, it's nearly impossible to go directly from feeling bad to feeling 100 percent good. But once you make something 10 percent better, it becomes easier to make it 20 percent better. Then it's easier to make it 40 percent better, and so on. Strive to make a bad situation a little better if you can, but if you can't, then make your *experience* of it better. For example, a common problem after intimate betrayal is the hard feelings of valued members of the betrayer's family. You can start out thinking of what might make the situation with, say, your ex-mother-in-law 10 percent better—perhaps sending her a sincerely written card or a flower as a kind of olive branch. If whatever you try doesn't improve the situation, change the way you experience it. In place of the self-denigrating interpretation that she's rejecting you or blaming you for the betrayal, see her as a hurt woman trying unsuccessfully to deal with her own pain. That doesn't excuse her behavior, but it improves your experience of it. Once again, we have no control over other people, but we have absolute control over the meaning of our experience. When we don't make the choice to improve the meaning we give to our experience, we're likely to repeat the same mistakes and feel the same pain over and over.

Keeping a log will help you focus on improving situations (or the way you experience them) in the future. Title this log "My Attempts to Improve Bad Situations," and use it to track the things you have done or will do to improve by 10 percent a bad situation or your experience of it. (Examples: I have tried to communicate respectfully, even when the other person is disrespectful; I enjoy music and recorded books while in traffic jams; I will try to solve problems rather than blaming them on others.)

Start out with a focus on relatively easy things to improve. As noted in Chapter 1, skills are more successfully acquired when initially practiced in relatively low-stress situations. In the beginning, practice improving situations—or your experience of situations—that are not directly related to the betrayal.

Keeping the "improve log" will help rewire your brain to think of ways to improve when something bad happens, rather than dwelling on how bad it is, which is likely to make it worse.

IMPROVEMENT EXERCISE

After practicing your improvement skills on less intense issues, try it with the following exercise: First, describe the hurt briefly; it's important to associate the desire to improve with a low-intensity experience of the hurt. Over time you will make the association automatically; that is, you will begin to look for ways to improve the situation or your experience of it when you feel bad.

Describe something that makes you feel depressed or resentful. *(Example: I can feel both when I think of how I believed my partner's assurances that he was working overtime when he was really with his lover.)*

Now describe what you can do to make your experience of the event or circumstance 10 percent better. *(Example: A trusting nature is an important part of who I am as a person. I will be more careful in the future about whom to trust and how much to trust, but I will not give anyone the power to change my nature.)*

Now describe what you can do to improve your experience of the event or circumstance 10 percent more. *(Example: Although my partner proved to be untrustworthy, there are ways I have benefited from trusting other people in my life—my children, my parents, friends, coworkers, casual acquaintances, even strangers on the street.)*

Now describe what you can do to improve your experience another 10 percent. *(Example: My trust in my best friend was rewarded by her support during my recovery process. I will send a note to tell her how much I appreciate her support.)*

Hopefully you noticed as you completed the above exercise that you felt more empowered with each step, through a slight shift in focus from the pain (and its causes) to improvement. Focus on improvement of any kind, regardless of whether it is directly related to the initial cause of your pain, will lessen the intensity of the hurt and, eventually, make it extinct.

Appreciate. We typically think of appreciation in terms of complimentary expressions such as "You're wonderful" (or "special," or "smart," or "attractive"). Yet expressions like these often feel hollow. That's because appreciation is primarily a felt condition, not a verbal one. Missing in most compliments is the essential component of appreciation—opening your heart and allowing yourself to be enhanced by certain qualities of other people or things. For example, when I appreciate your fine work or your thoughtful gestures, I am enhanced; I become a better person as long as I appreciate you. (This is why appreciating and being appreciated are so appealing in relationships: both parties become better.) What's more, my appreciation of you has a ripple effect—it helps me appreciate the beauty of the sunset, the drama of the painting, or the excitement of the movie or play.

In general, you'll achieve more growth by finding something to appreciate in a difficult relationship than in a benign one. For instance, Silvie had a mother who criticized everything from her parenting style to her choice of clothes and hairdo. It seemed that every encounter with her mother, by phone or in person, left Silvie understandably angry, initially at her mother, then at herself for needing her mother's help with the financial crisis that resulted from the breakup of her marriage. Her anger would eventually give way to guilt for devaluing her mother, followed by feelings of powerlessness and depressed mood. I worked with Silvie on compassionately asserting how she wanted her mother to treat her. (I'll cover compassionate assertiveness in Chapter 9.) We worked on developing appreciation of certain things about her mother; for example, the woman really did care about her, wanted what was best for her, and sacrificed time and money to help her.

As it turned out, Silvie's mother was quite moved to learn that her only daughter truly appreciated her, and her awareness of that allowed her to hear and respond positively to Silvie's description of how she wanted to be treated. But even if compassionate assertiveness had been unsuccessful and her mother had become defensive or remained critical, Silvie would have reaped the benefits of appreciation, because it detoxified most her thoughts about her mother. The ultimate issue isn't whether people deserve your negative thoughts; certainly many people do. The more important point is that they are *your* thoughts in *your* head, and you want them to be as beneficial to you as possible.

It's impossible to appreciate and feel devalued at the same time. As long as you appreciate, you will not feel devalued, as the following exercise should indicate.

APPRECIATION EXERCISE

The goal of this exercise is to open your heart to appreciation when you feel hurt. First, describe the hurt briefly; it's important to associate the desire to appreciate with a low-intensity experience of the hurt. You will notice over time that you will make the association automatically; in other words, you will begin to look for ways to appreciate someone or something when you feel bad.

Describe something that makes you blue or resentful. *(Examples: Holidays are especially hard, as I think about how my life was before the betrayal; I'm embarrassed that my marriage problems have affected my job; I can't concentrate or work as efficiently as I used to.)*

Now write down three things to appreciate about the room you are in at this moment. Force yourself, if necessary, to focus on your surroundings. *(Example: I have a lovely view of a lake from the room I'm in; the fireplace gives a sense of warmth, even though there is no fire burning right now; and the ceiling slopes gently, giving the room a peaceful quality.)*

Write down three things to appreciate about your job or the work you do in or around your home. *(Example: My job gives me a chance to feel productive; I make an* *important contribution; and I learn a great deal about people in my work.)*

Write down three things to appreciate about the time of year. *(Example: I love the crisp air in the morning, the stillness and quiet at night, and the excitement of small children as the holidays approach.)*

List three things to appreciate about your best friend. *(Example: My best friend has an incredibly kind heart; she is sensitive to the misfortunes of other people; and she improves the world in small ways through her caring.)*

List three things to appreciate about your parents or other elders in your life. *(Example: My father was highly intelligent with a wonderful sense of humor; my aunt was always kind to me; my boss has been understanding as I deal with my relationship difficulties.)*

List three things to appreciate about your children or other people, animals, or even plants you care for. *(Example: My daughter is the most intelligent person I know; my dog is so loving; my garden gives me peace.)*

List three things to appreciate about anything else.

Now read what you have written aloud.

Hopefully you noticed that, even when unrelated to what caused your emotional injury, appreciation invokes your core value and increases, at least slightly, your sense of meaning and purpose. If you look for something to appreciate whenever you feel down, you'll retrain your heart in the ways of healing and growth.

Remember, the harder it is to appreciate someone, the greater the reward. But if you get stuck, start by practicing on people who are easy to appreciate—Mother Teresa, Gandhi, Martin Luther King, and so forth.

Protect. Love activates a powerful instinct to protect. Indeed, self-value tends to rise and fall on the ability to protect loved ones. (In general, we feel more valuable when we protect them and less valuable when we fail to protect them.) Suppression of the instinct to protect also suppresses the ability to love. More to the point, it is hardly possible to heal any pain associated with betrayed love without following the instinct to protect other loved ones.

If you cannot protect loved ones through overt behavior (due to inaccessible or damaged relationships), do it in your imagination, in the knowledge that, at some point, you must make the effort to enact protective behavior in order to overcome the negative effects of intimate betrayal.

PROTECTION EXERCISE

Do this exercise whenever you need to access your core value. The most enduring sense of empowerment comes from exercising your natural instinct to protect. First, describe the hurt briefly; it's important to associate the desire to protect with a low-intensity experience of the hurt.

> **List three ways you protect those you love and care for.**
> (Example: I do everything I can to ensure their physical and psychological health; I let them know that I am always there for them; I don't hold their mistakes against them.)

You probably noticed in filling out the above that protecting loved ones—or imagining that you do—is empowering, certainly more so than devaluing yourself and others. As long as you're protective, you're unlikely to feel devalued, inadequate, or unlovable.

Connect. Connection is a sense that some part of your emotional world is also part of someone else's. It's transcendent, in that it makes us rise above purely selfish and petty concerns to regard the well-being of significant others or communities. On a biological level, connection elevates blood levels of the bonding hormone, oxytocin, which makes us feel calm, safe, and secure.

Connection is a mental state and a choice. You choose to feel connected to certain people or communities and you choose to feel disconnected from them. For the purpose of accessing your core value, the choice to feel connected can even be independent of a relationship; in other words, you can feel connected unilaterally. (I'll explore "attitudes of connection" as a way of jointly enriching relationships in a later chapter. The point here is to access core value, not necessarily to improve relationships.) To advance healing and growth, you can choose any level of connection: *intimate* (lovers or very close friends), familial, communal, or spiritual. Any level of connection will dispel the sense of isolation that prolongs suffering after intimate betrayal. Try writing down one thing that you can do that will help you feel connected on each of the above levels, remembering that connection is a mental state and a choice.

Core Value as Incompatible Response Strategy

One of the most potent of behavioral interventions is known as *incompatible response strategy* (Baron 1984). It's based on the principle that all organisms (including human beings) are incapable of engaging in two incompatible responses at once. It assumes one of the earliest of behavior principles: Where attention goes, behavior follows. The strategy is to focus attention on doing something that is incompatible with what you don't want to do. For example, you won't be successful for very long if you try to stop yelling at work or at home. The frustration of trying to suppress the impulse to yell while focused on *not* yelling will likely make you yell more. That's because the brain cannot do negatives; it must do something *instead* of what you don't want to do. If you practice speaking to others respectfully, with sensitivity to their individual sensibilities, you will not yell at them and are far more likely to get cooperation from them. Most of the exercises in this book are based on using core value as an incompatible response strategy to accomplish what you want to do—increase the value of your experience—instead of what you don't want to do—devalue yourself or others.

Of course, no single enactment of an incompatible response strategy will make a big difference in how you see yourself and others. But practice of the strategy over time will produce a huge positive change, as it literally rewires your brain to think in terms of healing, improving, appreciating, connecting, and protecting—all of which bring more value and meaning into your life.

EXERCISE

Be sure to perform the behaviors you describe below with conviction: "I am doing the right thing by acting on my deeper values." (If you approach all the exercises in the rest of the book with this attitude, and then enact the behaviors you describe, you will heal, improve, and grow.)

Describe something about your betrayal that invokes a state of numbness, nervousness, resentment, depression, or aggression. *(Example: I can feel all of these when I recall reading the e-mails my wife exchanged with her lover, in which they graphically described their lovemaking.)*

Describe what you can do to:

1. **Improve the situation or the way you experience it.**
    (Example: I will write many, many e-mails—more than I will actually send—to people I love, expressing my care and compassion for them. Over time, my thoughts con-

cerning e-mails will begin to symbolize expressions of love and compassion.)

2. **Appreciate.** *(Example: I will visit my favorite art gallery or mountain lake. I like myself more when I appreciate something than when I devalue my wife or anyone else.)*

3. **Protect.** *(Example: I will take my pet to the vet to see about her cough. I like myself better when I feel protective than when I feel destructive; protecting those I value is more important to me than devaluing.)*

4. **Connect.** *(Example: I will take some member of my family or a friend to dinner. Strengthening connections with loved ones over time will make the disconnection from my wife less important.)*

The above exercise once again demonstrates a crucial point about emotional healing and growth. While we cannot change what happened to us in the past, we have absolute control over the *meaning* of our lives in the present and future.

Think of the things that have the profoundest influence on our lives and how little control we have over them. We didn't choose our parents; we didn't sit down with God and say, "I'll take those two over there!" We didn't choose what illnesses our mothers suffered during pregnancy or whether they smoked or took aspirin. We didn't decide how much money our families would have, what early childhood illnesses or accidents we would experience, which schools we would go to, what kind of teachers and peers we would find there, whether other children would like or bully us.

We simply have no control over the major influences on our lives, yet we have absolute control over what they mean to us. If we define the meaning of our lives by bad things that happened to us, we create chronic states of powerlessness and resentment, with intermittent depression. If we define the meaning of our lives by systematically increasing the value of our experience, we create a life of meaning, purpose, and personal power.

The next chapter shows how to choose to act on your core value under stress or in the midst of anxious or depressed mood.

Summary

Your core value—your ability to create value and meaning in your life—is the key to healing and growth. You can access states of core value in various ways, such as by acting according to the most important thing about you as a person, or by trying to improve or appreciate or protect or connect. The more you access your core value, the stronger it becomes. The stronger it becomes, the more healing and growth you realize.

CHAPTER 6

Getting to Core Value under Pressure: Your Core Value Bank

This chapter will show how to build your "core value bank" (CVB)—a repository of the most important things to you and about you—and how to use it for healing and growth. The idea is to internalize concrete images of your core value that can serve as a place within, where you can go at any time, under any kind of stress, anxiety, or depressed mood to revitalize your desire to create value and meaning in your life.

After a few weeks of daily deposits to your CVB, the world around you will begin to remind you of your core value. For example, when you see a sunset, it will not only seem beautiful in and of itself; it will help you access your core value, for the sunset has value to you only because you have created it. The sunset will reinforce your deeper motivations to improve, appreciate, protect, or connect, and will greatly advance your goals of healing and growth.

The following are instructions for creating a CVB chart on a piece of paper and filling in the individual "safe-deposit boxes." Once it is filled out, I'll show how to use it as an invaluable tool for healing and growth.

Building Your CVB

You may have inferred from the last chapter that creating value is more psychologically relevant than the specific values you create. In terms of emotional healing and growth, the most significant factors are not your values per se, but whether you honor or violate them. Honoring brings a sense of conviction and authenticity. Violating brings guilt, shame, and anxiety.

Like all psychological drives, core value is a product of the naturally hierarchical processing of our brains, which necessarily makes some things more important than others. While all values are, by definition, important, states of core value concern what is *most* important. Remaining focused on your deepest values will strengthen your core value and accelerate healing and growth.

While many values are cultural and individual, your deepest values are likely to fall into the categories that were significant in the evolution of our species, as noted in a previous chapter. These types of values have been important to humans for tens of thousands of years: basic humanity, attachment (love), spirituality, creativity, compassionate behavior, and some degree of connection with nature and communities of people. They can serve as the safe-deposit boxes of your CVB.

Safe-Deposit Boxes

There are eight sections of the CVB. You can think of each as a safe-deposit box containing statements, images, or icons of the various ways you create value.

Divide a piece of paper into eight boxes, write each heading in its corresponding box, and fill in the boxes according to the instructions below. Don't worry that you're stronger in some boxes than in others. In general, people excel in two or three, and are weaker in the others. You can choose to develop any box at any time.

Box 1: Basic Humanity

Basic humanity is our innate interest in the well-being of others. In its more developed expressions, it motivates cooperative, respectful, helpful, nurturing, protective, and altruistic behaviors. In adversity, it motivates sacrifice and rescue. Most experts agree that these kinds of behaviors helped our earliest ancestors survive harsh environments and prevail in competition with more powerful predators.

Developing a sense of basic humanity allows us to grow beyond the limitations of personal experience and the prejudice that goes with it. The more in touch with basic humanity we are, the more humane we feel. When out of touch with it, we feel less humane, with diminished capacity for healing and growth.

The content of safe-deposit box 1 is an example of basic humanity drawn from reality or from your imagination. Here's the example I use with most of my clients:

Imagine that you're driving by yourself late at night, with only one other car on the road. Suddenly that car veers off the road and crashes into a tree. Two people are in the car, a mother and a four-year-old child. The mother is unhurt, but she's trapped in the front seat and will have to wait for a rescue team to pry open the twisted metal and deployed air bags that have trapped her. She cannot help her little girl, who climbs out the back window. Though not physically harmed, the child, startled awake by the crash and unable to see her mother, feels helpless and panicky. She shivers with fear. You are the only one who can help. What will you do?

Of course, most people would call 911, reassure the mother that help is on the way, and comfort the child.

Imagine that you've done the first two, and now you're comforting the child. Close your eyes (it's easier to imagine when your eyes are closed) and feel yourself comforting this frightened child. You're hugging her, rocking her, whispering to her, encouraging her. You're trying so hard to comfort the frightened child that it takes a moment to realize how well it's working. She's calming down, holding tightly onto you, her head on your chest. You feel her heart beating with your heart. She feels soothed, peaceful, and good, due to you—your caring and your compassion.

(I like this example because comforting a desperate, innocent child invokes our instincts to improve, appreciate, protect, and connect simultaneously. You can, of course, come up with something else that invokes your sense of basic humanity and describe that instead.)

Box 2: Meaning and Purpose

Meaning and purpose are not, strictly speaking, values. They result from being true to the most important things to and about us. If we are true to our deeper values, whatever they are, we have a sense of meaning and purpose. If we're not, we don't, and we're likely to fill the void with obsessions or addictions, or simply become lethargic, with little motivation and vitality. I include meaning and purpose here only to make them more accessible to consciousness. Otherwise, we tend to think in terms of meaning and purpose only when we've lost them.

Your CVB uses two statements to reflect in miniature the meaning and purpose of your life. The first statement to write down is whatever is the *most* important thing about you as a person. Although you've already written this in the last chapter, write it again in box 2. (Repetition is the easiest way yet discovered to retrain the brain.)

The second statement describes the most important thing about your life in general. Think in terms of your legacy to the world or how you would like to be remembered. This is what you would like on your tombstone, or in a one- or two-sentence eulogy.

Box 3: Attachment (Love)

Attachment is the formation and maintenance of affectionate bonds. It's the first value we create in life. Attachment pain tends to be the worst kind of emotional pain, which is why intimate betrayal is so devastating—it can make you feel unlovable and inadequate as an intimate partner, parent, child, sibling, or close friend.

Fill this box with the names of your loved ones. You're writing their names, but the actual content of the box is the love you have for them.

Box 4: Spirituality

In the psychological sense, spirituality is not necessarily about God or religion. It is a sense of connection to something larger than the self. That something can be God; nature; the cosmos; a social, moral, or political cause; or the sea of humanity. The importance of spiritual connection predates recorded history. Evidence suggests that the Neanderthals—the more primitive group of "cave men"—buried their dead in what appear to have been spiritual ceremonies (Maureille 2002).

In this box, add a symbol (a drawing or mark or word will do) of something that has spiritual significance to you. It can be religious, natural, cosmic, or social, connecting you to something larger than the self.

Box 5: Nature

The ability to appreciate and be moved by the beauty of nature seems to be uniquely human. We are capable of admiring nature and feeling a part of it at the same time. (Interestingly, when movie directors want to give animals or robots human qualities—such as in *Wall-E* and the most recent remake of *King Kong*—they show the robots or animals admiring the beauty of nature.)

In this safe-deposit box, name, draw, or describe a nature scene that strikes you as beautiful. Note: In this and in the next box, concentrate on things you're likely to see in your environment. The Taj Mahal and the gardens of Babylon are fine, but you need lots of local beauty for ongoing core value reinforcement.

Box 6: Creativity

Creativity includes the expression and appreciation of art, literature, architecture, music, dance, furniture, jewelry, or anything created by you or by another person. Both creating and appreciating will access core value, to a degree commensurate with the effort and energy you put into the activity. Most of the time, creating requires more effort and energy, but avid appreciation will also deliver substantial reward.

In this safe-deposit box, identify a piece of art, music, craft, or architecture, or another human creation that you value.

Box 7: Community

A conscious sense of community occurs with the realization that you are connected to a group of people. The human brain developed to its present form when we still needed to live in tightly-knit communities to survive. The biological importance of community is seen in the high degree of communal contagion of emotions—a powerful, unconscious force underlying social structure (Hatfield, Cacioppo, and Rapson 1994). In other words, the social transmission and reception of emotions includes us in communities, both large and small, whether or not we are aware of them. Core value is accessed when we make ourselves aware of them.

In this box, identify how or where you experience community connection—for example, place of worship, school, work, or neighborhood.

Box 8: Compassion

The definition of a compassionate act is something that helps relieve the suffering, hardship, or discomfort of another person, with no material gain to you. In other words, you do not do it to get something in return. Compassionate acts are the lubricant of social bonds and the lifeblood of intimate relationships. It's almost certain that you felt a significant decrease in compassion from your partner prior to the betrayal.

Psychologically speaking, there is more reward from small but frequent compassionate behaviors than from a few large ones. Giving a dollar to charity whenever you can, for example, carries more accumulative psychological reward than giving a lump sum at Christmastime. There is no act of compassion too small to access a state of core value. Anything that fits into a routine is more likely to produce lasting change and significant benefit.

In safe-deposit box 8, list three compassionate things you have done. These are times you helped or comforted someone else, with no material gain to you. The content of the box is your emotional state when you perform small gestures of compassion. (Choose relatively small gestures that can be part of your routine—helping someone struggling with packages, visiting the sick, talking to someone who feels down.)

Using Your CVB

The rest of this chapter will describe three different ways to use your CVB for general healing and growth:

- daily investment—training your brain to think in terms of creating value and meaning

- restorative images—healing painful memories (as discussed in Chapter 4)

- emotion regulation—calming you down when you're upset and cheering you up when you're down

Daily investment. A primary purpose of making daily investments in your CVB is to relieve the stress that accumulates from chronically devaluing yourself and others, a tendency that almost always follows intimate betrayal. The long-term goal is to create a habit of value creation, so you will automatically seek to increase the value of your experience. Hence a strategy with unmatched potential for psychological healing is to add one new item to your CVB, or enhance an item already in it, every day for the rest of your life.

If that seems like too much, just do it on the days when you eat. That's not entirely a joke; you want to think of core value work as replenishment, something that must be done every day, like eating and sleeping. It doesn't take a lot of time, only a few seconds really, yet the daily repetition rewires the brain to think and act in terms of building value rather than devaluing.

The "nature" and "creative" boxes are the most accessible to new items, as there are many thousands of possibilities. The other boxes require mindfulness, appreciation, and practice of what is already in the boxes, rather than addition of new items. Be more mindful of your basic humanity connections, of the meaning and purpose of your life, of the love you have for significant others. Appreciate your spiritual and community connections, as well as the small compassionate acts you perform.

CORE VALUE BANK DAILY INVESTMENT STATEMENT

Your core value bank is open night and day for deposits. At any given moment, you can do something—or remind yourself that you have done something—to access your core value and move further along the path of healing and growth. Of course, overt behavior has the biggest effect on brain processing, but imagining behavior will produce a positive effect, if repeated over time.

Keep track of your "credits" by copying and filling out the following list on a piece of paper.

Number of times today that I helped someone:

Number of times I respected someone:

Number of times I (silently) valued people I passed on the street:

Number of times I valued people I talked to on the phone.

Number of times I felt self-compassion (recognized my hurt with motivation to improve and heal):

Number of times I felt compassion for someone else (understood her perspective and offered to help):

Number of times I felt love for someone:

Number of times I felt an intimate connection:

Number of times I felt a communal connection:

Number of times I felt a spiritual connection:

Number of times I improved (by at least 5 percent) a troublesome situation, or improved my experience of it:

Number of times, when I worried about something bad that might happen, I thought of how to improve it if it does happen:

Number of times I appreciated something about someone:

Number of times I appreciated something in nature:

Number of times I appreciated something made by a person—music, art, architecture, furniture, clothing, and so forth:

Number of times I acted according to my deepest values:

Number of times I felt protective of someone, while respecting his autonomy:

Number of times I renewed my purpose in life:

Credit total:

The "credit total" above is meant as a way of giving yourself credit for exercising your core value. Keeping track of the daily balance of your CVB Investment Statements will offer a relatively objective, quantitative appraisal of your progress in healing and growth.

Although the power of core value lies in the ability to control the meaning of your experience in the present, it also gives a perspective on the lifelong task of creating value and meaning. On a separate sheet of paper, fill out the following list once every other month. For each item on the list, answer "some," "a lot," or "an enormous number/amount." You should notice significant movement over time—from small numbers to larger ones.

Lifetime Core Value Bank Statement

Number of people I have helped:

Amount of suffering in the world I have decreased:

Moments of happiness I have caused:

Number of small ways I have made the world a better place (you can use your CVB daily statement as a guide):

Restorative images. As you fill up the safe-deposit boxes of your CVB over time, you simultaneously build a supply of restorative images, any one of which can be associated with painful memories for the purpose of healing them, in the manner described in Chapter 4. Your CVB is a repository of restorative images.

Emotion regulation. In its simplest form, emotion regulation is calming yourself down when you're upset and cheering yourself up and when you're down. In general, we get upset and feel down when we perceive (usually unconsciously) some type of hurt or vulnerability. The most common forms of hurt and vulnerability that cause emotion dysregulation are feeling disregarded, guilty, rejected, powerless, inadequate, or unlovable. Emotion regulation occurs when we move from states of hurt and vulnerability to states of core value. The underlying strategy of most the exercises in this book is to convert hurt and vulnerability into empowered states of core value.

A streamlined version of your CVB (one image per safe-deposit box) is a useful aid in reversing any maladaptive defenses against vulnerability that may have formed since the betrayal. (It also works with insomnia, which I'll address in the next chapter.) You'll recall from Chapter 3 that Cindy was having an especially hard time recovering from her husband's multiple affairs. Like many of my clients, she resisted commitment to a healing identity at first. But once she made the commitment, she was able to use her CVB to heal her hurt. Her assignment was to set aside five-minute practice sessions 12 times per day. (That number seems to be optimal for forming emotional habits, though, of course, it varies with individual cases.) In each practice session, she thought about the affairs, just long enough to stimulate feelings of inadequacy or unlovability. As soon as she got into the painful feeling, she ran through each box of her CVB. She imagined comforting the desperate child. She recalled the most important thing about her as a person—that she was caring, compassionate, and loving to the people she loved. She remembered the most important thing about her life in general, which was to contribute as much kindness to the world as she could. She felt her love for the significant people in her life—her children, parents, aunts, and two best friends. She felt her connection to her God. She felt awe at the autumn leaves of her imagination. She felt her favorite music, the camaraderie of her labor union, and a series of small compassionate things she had done. The repetition of this process forged a solid connection between states of hurt and vulnerability and her core value, so that every time she felt inadequate or unlovable, her core value was automatically activated, proving to her that she is, indeed, valuable and lovable, *because* she values and loves. Within two weeks of practice, she deeply believed this crucial fact: her core value is far more important than her partner's bad behavior.

We'll follow Cindy's progress to full healing and growth in future chapters.

EMOTION REGULATION EXERCISE

The exercise below is designed to help you associate intrusive thoughts with images from your CVB. With practice, the occurrence of the former will stimulate the latter. Practice sessions consist of recalling an unpleasant thought, then running through a streamlined version of your CVB. Most of the time, this practice will help you arrive at something you can do to improve the situation or your experience of it.

Describe something you resent about your betrayal.
(Example: My ex stole most of the money from our retirement plan, yet she demands an equal share of what remains in our divorce settlement.)

Invoke the emotions of your CVB. *(Do it mentally or write down just one item for each category: Basic Humanity, Meaning and Purpose, Attachment, Spirituality, Nature, Creativity, Community, and Compassion.)*

Explain what you will do to improve. *(Example: I will pursue my legal recourse for a fairer settlement, but I will not obsess about it or internalize my ex's violation of her core value. Instead, I will improve situations the best I can, appreciate as much as I can, connect to loved ones, identify with my community, exercise my spiritual values, and be as compassionate as I can be.)*

Describe something about your betrayal that makes you feel depressed or anxious. *(Example: He mistreated me throughout our marriage and I put up with it.)*

Invoke the emotions of your CVB. *(Do it mentally or write down just one item per category: Basic Humanity, Meaning and Purpose, Attachment, Spirituality, Nature, Creativity, Community, and Compassion.)*

Explain what you will do to improve. *(Example one: I stayed in a bad marriage because I wanted to keep my family intact. That was a noble goal. I have confidence in my core value, specifically that it will help me trust more wisely in the future. Example two: I stayed in a bad marriage because I was afraid to leave and face my dread of isolation. I will build a social network of friends and family to ward off the natural feelings of isolation that occur when attachment relationships are ending. I will develop my core value by focusing my thoughts, feelings, and behavior on improving, appreciating, protecting, and connecting.)*

Repeat the emotion regulation exercise above with different items that make you feel depressed, anxious, or resentful, until you gain confidence that, no matter how down, distressed, angry, or resentful you might be, if you saw a desperate child, you would stop being down, distressed, resentful, or angry and go to the child to comfort her and calm her. Practice until you are confident that, under stress, you can renew the meaning and purpose of your life by reinforcing the most important thing about you as a person and the most important thing about your life. Practice until you know that when you're under stress you can get in touch with your love for the significant people in your life, feel your spiritual connection, and appreciate beauty in nature and creative endeavors. Practice until you feel confident that, under stress, you can feel your community connection and remember small compassionate things you have done. With practice, you will be able to improve any situation you encounter—or at least improve your experience of what you encounter. You will heal and grow. You will control the meaning of your life.

Your CVB will be the foundation of a strategy to deal with the post-traumatic stress symptoms that almost always emerge during recovery from intimate betrayal. Overcoming those symptoms is the subject of the next chapter.

Summary

Your core value bank is an internal repository of the most important things to and about you. It has eight safe-deposit boxes with images, icons, and statements in the broad categories of values that, to some degree, are nearly universal among human beings. It has an expansive quality—becoming ever larger with new items and enhancements on a daily basis—and it helps retrain your heart in the ways of healing and growth. In a streamlined version, it can aid in emotion regulation, calming you down when you're upset, cheering you up when you're down, and, as you'll see in the next chapter, helping you sleep when sleep doesn't come easily.

CHAPTER 7

Intimate Betrayal and Post-Traumatic Stress

As if recovery from intimate betrayal weren't hard enough, nature has to complicate it further by throwing in symptoms of post-traumatic stress (PTS), which most betrayed people will experience to some extent. This chapter will describe PTS and show how to manage its more intrusive symptoms.

The most familiar type of PTS—the one that gets most of the press—is caused by an acute stressor, or life-threatening event, which exerts an extreme reaction in the central nervous system (CNS). Examples are military combat, rape, mugging, gun violence, or a serious car crash.

The other type of post-traumatic stress is caused by less intense but longer lasting stressors, often suffered by people who are sued, put on trial for crimes, investigated by the Internal Revenue Service, persecuted, discriminated against, bullied, or ridiculed at work or school. This kind of stressor does not invoke significant fear of harm or annihilation. Instead, it brings a terrible dread of shame, humiliation, and isolation or loss of status and resources, if not personal freedom. It keeps the CNS at a chronic level of heightened stress. Intimate betrayal typically invokes this kind of PTS response.

A Physiological Model

I use the following physiological model to explain the kind of PTS that typically follows intimate betrayal, because the initial CNS reaction is more physiological than psychological in nature. Suppose you're alone in a room, and one of the columns holding the ceiling begins to list perilously. The only way to save yourself is to prop up the column with your shoulder until help arrives. About twenty-four hours later, help comes to secure the column and prop up the ceiling, safely relieving you of the burden. When you try to walk away, you are unable to straighten up and walk normally. The overexerted nerve endings in your shoulder, side, and leg muscles have paralyzed the tissue around them, temporarily rendering key muscles nearly immobile. The condition gradually eases. Within about three days, you can finally stand up straight and enjoy full mobility. But for another three days or so, you experience occasional muscle spasms in your shoulder, side, and legs, where most of the stress was concentrated. These are rough estimates of recovery time that do not allow for variations in age, health, muscle tone, or flexibility, but you get the idea—prolonged stress necessitates a prolonged recovery process.

A similar condition occurs with long-term emotional stressors, such as walking on eggshells in your home, living with continual criticism or contempt, or harboring suspicions of deceit, infidelity, or embezzlement by an intimate partner. Once the stressor has finally passed—the betrayal is exposed and the subsequent free-fall condition has abated—the CNS does not return to normal for quite some time. (Precisely how long depends on the duration of the stressful conditions and the level of determination to focus on healing, repairing, and improving.) The entire system must recalibrate to find a normal range of arousal, without the chronic stressor "pressing" against it.

The mental equivalent of muscle spasms during the CNS recalibration process is experienced as waves of negative emotion, which seem to come out of nowhere, with little or no warning. Often with no discernible trigger, waves of emotion seize control of your body, which becomes tense, rigid, and agitated. They dominate your consciousness and make it seem like you're incapable of thinking about anything other than how terrible you feel or how awful your partner is for making you feel so bad. They typically start with a flash point—an abrupt awareness that you're about to experience something horrid. A physical marker sometimes occurs with the flash point, something like a pit in your stomach, a sharp pain, muscular weakness, or blurred vision.

Here are the most common symptoms that come in waves during the recovery process:

- vivid flashbacks of painful incidents from the past (often from childhood)

- intense anxiety or fear

- utter confusion and impaired decision-making

- rage

- sorrow, hopelessness, depression, or despair

- high impulsivity

- aggressive or violent fantasies

Triggers and Timing of the Symptoms

PTS symptoms have triggers, but they are often difficult and sometimes impossible to discern. Once again, physical pain is a useful model of how the triggers work and why they're so hard to figure out.

The brain processes pain on a dedicated neural network that gets priority processing. If you doubt that, imagine this: During a soulful, mutually validating talk with your best friend, you spill hot coffee on yourself. What do you think your brain will regard as more important, paying attention to your friend or attending to your injury? After the burn, priority neural networks become hypersensitive. You flinch when your hand gets near a hot cup of coffee, because the pain has been associated with the heat. This involuntary reaction persists until repeated experience over time demonstrates that pain caused by the hot coffee is unlikely to recur, as long as you're careful.

Just as sensing heat triggers the flinch in the burn victim's hand, the reinstatement of intimacy, trust, love, or compassion can trigger the same kind of involuntary "flinch"—waves of negative emotions—after intimate betrayal. It is intimacy that led to betrayal, and the betrayed brain will likely associate pain with intimate exposure. Because feelings of intimacy are often vague, with a wide range of associated memories (from toddlerhood, all the way through your most recent experience), specific triggers of PTS responses are hard to pinpoint. But you can bet that in the months following intimate betrayal, the alarm will sound at the most inopportune time—during a warm embrace with a friend, or in a moment of enjoyment with your children, or in the midst of pleasant thoughts. Out of nowhere, the waves of negative emotions will crash upon you.

Cindy's path to recovery was strewn with more than a few PTS episodes. They came at work and while helping her children with school assignments, especially when she began to make progress in her attempts to repair her marriage. The worst incident happened when she and her husband were on vacation at their honeymoon spot in the Bahamas. He had been so sorry for his actions and had tried so hard to repair their marriage that she was willing to try a second honeymoon. They were walking on the beach, feeling the warm breezes from the gentle sea. She felt closer to him than she had in years. Suddenly, her body went rigid. It started as a pit in her stomach and flashed throughout her body like hot beams of light—a moving, consuming anger. She could remember nothing—no thoughts, images, or sounds—only the burning edge of rage.

"You've ruined everything!" she screamed at her husband. "You've ruined my life! You selfish prick! You goddamn, selfish bastard!" She didn't care that other people on the beach were staring at her. She had to get away from him. She ran all the way back to the hotel, her anger giving her the energy to run at least two miles in the thick sand.

She chain-locked the door of their hotel room so he couldn't get in. He called weakly from the hallway, asking if he could help. She couldn't stop thinking about his lies. She hated him. But she also hated herself for hating him.

Gradually, her anger abated, and she dropped into a bottomless despair.

"What's wrong with me?" she cried. "My life is much better now. I have everything I've ever wanted, and I'm more miserable than ever. What is *wrong* with me?"

You Are Not Your Symptoms

It's important to know that PTS symptoms are not part of your personality. They are merely a delayed, mostly physiological, response to past stressors. They are a perfectly natural stage of recovery from a prolonged period of stress.

The most damaging aspect of PTS symptoms are *secondary symptoms,* or symptoms about symptoms. Secondary symptoms are triggered by the meaning you give to primary symptoms. If you think the abrupt waves of emotion mean that you're crazy, or that you will never be well or happy, or that you're defective or dying, then the effects are horrible, and you get flooded with adrenaline and cortisol from the secondary symptoms on top of the primary ones.

To heal and grow, as you so richly deserve to do, you must control the meaning of your emotional experience—in other words, what it means to you and about you. That is the secret of managing the intrusive symptoms of PTS that so often follow intimate betrayal.

How to Manage the Symptoms

Handle the waves of PTS feelings with gentleness and care. There is good news in them. Their very existence means that the stressor has been removed. No one has nightmares about bombs dropping *during* the war. While stressors are active, the CNS goes into survival mode, with no mental resources allotted to "getting back to normal." Only after the stressor is over does the CNS begin to recalibrate to normal. That is why a diagnosis of post-traumatic stress disorder (PTSD) cannot be made until at least three months after the stressor has been removed.

More good news:

- The symptoms are *temporary*. Unless you feed them with speculation about why they're occurring or what they mean about you or your present relationships, they will last no more than a few minutes.

- They are a sign of healing.

- They're not about now; they're residual effects of something that happened in the past.

The best way to handle the waves of negative emotion is to sit back and let them wash over you. Say to yourself, "Oh, here's one of those temporary waves. It doesn't mean anything, and it will soon pass. I'm okay now, and I'll be better in a few minutes."

The symptoms are a lot like waves at the beach. If you try to stand up to crashing ocean waves, they can grind you into the sand. But if you dive under them, you're aware only of a force whooshing quickly over you. Allow the PTS symptoms to wash over you like the sensation of swimming under waves at the beach. Then they will last no more than a few minutes, with minimal discomfort. Managed in this way, they will most likely diminish in frequency and intensity until they stop altogether.

Moving through your core value bank (CVB) during the waves of emotions is another way to shorten their duration. That night in the hotel room where she had gone with her cheating husband for a second honeymoon, Cindy finally remembered the PTS training we had practiced in her therapy. She remembered that her symptoms required gentleness and care. She told herself that the symptoms were temporary, without psychological meaning; they were merely a physiological response, like muscle spasms, a residual effect of past events and a signal that she was in a healing process that would soon be completed. She associated the symptoms with her core value bank. She imagined comforting the desperate child. She recalled the most important thing about her as a person: that she was caring, compassionate, and loving to the people she loved. She remembered the most important thing about her life in general, which was to contribute as much kindness to the world as she could. She felt her love for the significant people in her life—her children, parents, aunts, and best friends. She felt her connection to her God, and her awe at the autumn leaves. She imagined her favorite music, the labor union she belonged to, and a series of small compassionate things she had done. By the time she was finished, her anger and despair were gone.

Cindy's waves of negative emotion came back three or four times over the next several weeks, though with less intensity. At the first flash point—for her it was the pit in her stomach—she managed her PTS episodes as described above. And then they were over.

CVB EXERCISE FOR PTS

Use this exercise to practice control of post-traumatic stress symptoms. On a separate piece of paper:

Describe a wave of negative emotion you've experienced that seemed to come out of nowhere.

Now imagine that during this experience, you are reassuring yourself that it is temporary, without psychological meaning, a mere physiological response, a residual effect to past events, and a signal that you are in a healing process that will soon be completed. Associate the images of your core value bank with the symptoms you experienced. As bad as the wave of feelings were, had you seen a desperate child, you would have crawled, if necessary, to help the child, because this is who you truly are. Feel yourself comforting the desperate child and growing stronger in the process. Remember the most important thing about you as a person and the most important thing about your life. Feel the love for the significant people in your life. Feel your spiritual connection, something beautiful in nature, something creative that moves you, your sense of community, and how you feel when you do small compassionate acts. Feel yourself grow stronger and larger than your temporary symptoms.

Practicing the above responses in your imagination while remembering past waves of emotion will make it easier to do the exercise when the waves come over you in real time. With practice, you will be able to manage the symptoms with gentleness and care, until they become extinct.

Medication

If your symptoms seem too intense to handle, or if you have any suicidal or self-harming thoughts, please seek a medication evaluation from a licensed psychiatrist. Think of it as psychiatric novocaine to help numb the pain while healing progresses, as you perform the techniques described above. (About 25 percent of my clients have found temporary medication helpful.) Seeking medical help when necessary is the kind of gentleness and care that is entirely consistent with your healing identity.

Insomnia

In the weeks following intimate betrayal, almost everyone suffers some kind of sleep disturbance. Once PTS takes hold, sleeping soundly seems like a faint memory of the distant past. The unfortunate result is impaired cognitive processes, low energy, and higher error rates in whatever you try to do. Our ability to regulate emotions and keep calm and reasonably optimistic under stress falters greatly with sleep deprivation. (The brain perceives more vulnerability when tired and is more likely to use the adrenaline of low-grade anger for energy. That's why irritability is a hallmark of sleep deprivation.) Most of my clients who suffer intimate betrayal begin treatment with one of the three forms of insomnia described below.

Normal sleep patterns consist of cycles that last about ninety minutes each. Insomnia typically intrudes at the start of a cycle or at the end of one. For example, Carl had *near-term* insomnia. It took him at least ninety minutes to three hours (one or two sleep cycles) to fall asleep. He'd toss and turn, struggling with thoughts of his wife's affair, for what seemed like interminably long periods of time before slipping into a restive sleep.

Josh had *end-term* insomnia. He'd wake up most mornings ninety minutes to three hours before his alarm clock went off. He didn't have enough energy to get up and start the day, nor did he have enough tranquility to fall back to sleep—not once his thoughts returned to his financial woes since his wife cleaned out their bank accounts, including their 401(k). After much worry, he'd finally doze off, only to be jarred awake by the morning alarm.

Elizabeth had the kind of sleep disturbance most likely to occur after intimate betrayal: *mid-term* insomnia. She'd fall asleep easily enough, but only for two to three hours. In the middle of the night she'd be wide awake anywhere from ninety minutes to four hours. Although she had finally left her emotionally abusive husband many months before, thoughts of his continual blame, name-calling, and criticism would arise during these early hours of the morning. The level of fatigue, especially the next afternoon, is no worse in this type of sleep dysfunction than the other two. But mid-term insomnia has a more potent effect on mood. Just a few weeks of this particular pattern of sleep disturbance can produce biological depression, possibly because it inhibits replenishment of the neurotransmitters responsible for regulating moods and, in general, feeling well.

Needless to say, all three of these clients had tried sleeping pills that helped for a short while. But all three, like most of my clients, found that medication didn't stop nighttime thoughts about their betrayal; it just made them a bit fuzzier and less coherent.

As we pass from wakefulness to sleep, predominant activity in the brain shifts from the left hemisphere to the right. The left hemisphere is more analytic, computational, and verbal, among other things, while the right hemisphere is more intuitive, sensuous, and imaginary. Here's an easy, though somewhat oversimplified, way to frame the distinction: The left brain thinks in language and numbers, while the right brain thinks in images and symbols. You may have noticed that Carl, Josh, and Elizabeth invariably thought in words and financial numbers when they awoke. This pattern greatly reduced their chances of falling quickly back to sleep. What's more, their thoughts produced anxiety and resentment, both of which involve biochemical stimulation of the central nervous system. Their tossing and turning, characteristic of all forms of insomnia, caused the secretion of another stimulant—cortisol—to energize tired muscles.

The healing strategy for all three forms of insomnia is to convert any words in your core value bank to images or pictures. Whenever they woke up, Carl, Josh, and Elizabeth tried to lie still and focus on their CVB images, which automatically led to other soothing images, nature photographs, and scenes from movies—no words, no numbers, no anxiety, only soothing images.

This strategy didn't work every time they woke up; sometimes they'd been dreaming in language and numbers or, worse, about the betrayal itself, and were already well behind the curve of biochemical stimulation. But most of the time, their CVBs helped them get a handle on their insomnia.

More insomnia tips. I give my insomniac clients the following guidelines, culled from a number of trends in sleep research and clinical advice from sleep experts:

- Keep your bedroom as dark as possible. Cover up the glowing digits of a clock radio and anything else electric. Darkness enhances the secretion of melatonin, the brain's natural sleep inducer.

- Go to bed and get up at the same time each day. We all have our own biological clocks of optimal sleeping and activity levels that function best when they are on a regular schedule.

- Reduce nicotine, caffeine, alcohol, and other stimulants, especially after 3 p.m., at least until your insomnia is gone.

- Limit naps to one short one per day, no more than twenty minutes.

- Exercise for thirty minutes a day—walking will do—but not within three hours of bedtime.

- Limit activities in bed. Don't work or watch TV or surf the web. Just sleep or have sex in your bed.

- Avoid late dinners and nightcaps. But a light snack of protein and carbohydrates (such as a couple of crackers with cheese or half a bowl of cereal with milk) helps many people sleep.

- Make your sleeping environment comfortable, dark, and quiet.

INSOMNIA EXERCISE

Collect pictures or draw images to represent one or two items of each safe-deposit box of your CVB. On a plain piece of paper, draw five vertical lines and three horizontal lines to form the eight safe-deposit boxes of your CVB. Paste each picture or drawing in its appropriate box and memorize the images. Whenever you can't get to sleep, lie perfectly still and meditate on the pictures, one by one, slowly passing in an endless loop in your imagination—no words, no numbers, no anxiety, only soothing images.

Summary

PTS symptoms are usual after suffering intimate betrayal. They are more physiological than psychological. They will do minimal harm and will last for a shorter period of time if you are able to manage the secondary symptoms, which come from giving the primary symptoms a negative meaning about yourself. With gentleness, care, and practice, they will not constitute a barrier to healing and growth. Instead, they will serve as an opportunity to reinforce your healing identity and your ability to access your core value under stress.

CHAPTER 8

How to Change Hidden Guilt and Shame into Self-Compassion

The greatest obstacles to healing and growth following intimate betrayal are also the cruelest, because they seem so unfair. In both hidden and overt ways, guilt and shame permeate the hurt of intimate betrayal and affect all close relationships. It would be highly unusual if at least one of your family or close relationships has not become problematic to some extent since the betrayal.

Guilt and shame operate mostly outside awareness—when you're conscious of them at all, it's usually in the form of regret or anxiety, which are reinforced by potent evolutionary and cultural pressures. The vast majority of the guilt and shame triggered by your partner's betrayal is irrational in nature; in other words, you didn't do anything to cause the guilt or shame.

First I'll define guilt and shame, and then I'll show why they present barriers to recovery from intimate betrayal. Guilt is an uncomfortable and often painful feeling that comes from the belief—implicit or explicit—that you have violated a personal standard through specific thoughts or behaviors; that is, you did (or imagined doing) something you regard as wrong. Shame is more global—a painful experience of the self as failing, due to character defect, inferiority, or inadequacy.

Our susceptibility to hidden and irrational guilt and shame after betrayal owes largely to the pattern-matching function of the brain, discussed in Chapter 1. The brain constantly tries to match present perceptions with emotions and motivations from past experience. When you're suffering emotional pain, pattern matching becomes less accurate. The effect is like opening a jack-in-the-box labeled, "rejection, failure, mistakes," at which point the guilt and shame that go with those past associations leap out at you. In other words, the brain tends to run lots of rejections, mistakes, and failures into implicit memory, if they seem remotely relevant to whatever is happening now. Since everyone has at least a little guilt and shame around past attachments, hidden guilt and shame are almost certain to occur after intimate betrayal.

Traditional psychotherapy could take years to pinpoint the supposed past causes of those various mental associations, with the goal of relieving residual guilt and shame that can cause anxiety, depression, and anger problems in the present. A much simpler alternative is to turn all guilt and shame—hidden and overt—into self-compassion, with the goal of accessing states of core value that facilitate healing and growth. That is the intention of this chapter.

The first step in turning guilt and shame into a force for healing and growth is to understand why they are so powerful, even when completely irrational.

Survival and Cultural Forces

As mentioned in Chapter 1, most anthropologists agree that early humans would not have survived without strong emotional bonds that made them cooperate in food gathering and territorial defense. Not surprisingly, modern humans are endowed with highly developed, preverbal, prerational, and automatic emotional inhibitions and reactions to behaviors that threaten emotional bonds. Fundamental to these reactions and inhibitions are guilt and shame, which create vulnerability—feeling bad and powerless—when attachment bonds are threatened. If I threaten the bond—in thought or deed—I experience guilt. If a loved one threatens it, I experience shame, commonly referred to as rejection. We usually encounter both at the same time. If I threaten the bond, my loved one is apt to reject me, thereby adding shame to the guilt; if my loved one threatens the bond, I may react by doing something that threatens it further, thereby adding guilt to the shame.

The vulnerability engendered by guilt and shame can be relieved by strengthening the attachment bond. This process—relieving threats to the bond by strengthening it—worked well for millennia, until we developed an ego. The modern human ego resists implicit suggestions of mistakes (guilt) and failure (shame). In modern times, guilt and shame are usually hidden beneath ego defenses of blame, anger, resentment, denial, and avoidance.

An example of how the ego undermines the natural function of guilt and shame is seen in what researchers call the "demand-withdrawal" dynamic (Eldridge and Christensen 2002). That's when one partner wants more closeness than the other can tolerate. The withdrawing party experiences guilt for his inability to meet the emotional needs of his partner and chooses an ego defense against the guilt, usually blame ("You're too needy!") or anger ("You're smothering me!") or avoidance ("Not now!"). The demanding party feels the shame of rejection, and is apt to use similar defenses of blame ("You're a cold, intimacy-avoider!") or anger ("You're abusing me!") or denial ("I know you really want to be close; it's just your childhood issues getting in the way!"). As long as they interact on the level of ego defenses, resolution of this standoff is impossible. The path to resolution relevant to this book is for both parties to regulate their guilt and shame with self-compassion, and access core value states to decide whether their connection is valuable enough to invest the energy and effort necessary to nurture it.

Cultural Reinforcement of Guilt and Shame

Throughout most of modern history, attachment bonds have been viewed as the cornerstone of stable, orderly, and cohesive communities. As a consequence, cultural mores and laws to protect the "sanctity" of the family have evolved (Coontz 2006). Although our notions of family are undergoing a cultural transformation now, you are still likely to encounter an unfair bias in many people, who will assume that you have responsibility, if not for the betrayal, then for the relationship distress that led to it. This tendency to "blame the victim" does two things for those who perpetrate it. First, it creates a vague hope that if both parties are to blame, reconciliation is more likely, and the family unit—as the presumed cornerstone of the culture—can be preserved. More personally, those who project this attitude naively believe that it protects them from betrayal by their intimate partners—if they don't make the same "mistakes," they will be safe.

This cultural bias is one of the reasons I spent so much time in Chapters 5 and 6 on developing core value. Your sense of who you are must come from your ability to create value and meaning in your life, and not from what other people, with their own psychological and cultural agendas, may think of you.

Guilt and Shame vs. Compassion for Self and Loved Ones

Compassion is sympathy for the hurt, distress, or vulnerability of another, with motivation to help. Self-compassion is a sympathetic response to your own hurt, distress, or vulnerability, with a motivation to heal, repair, and improve. At heart, both are simple appreciation of the basic human frailty we all share. The experience of compassion for someone else makes you feel more humane and less isolated and often serves as a jump-start to self-compassion.

The lists below highlight the differences between guilt and shame on the one hand and compassion on the other.

Unregulated Guilt and Shame	Compassion
Block core value and obstruct interpersonal bridges	Invokes core value and reinstates interpersonal bridges
Fuel anger, resentment, or depression	Is incompatible with anger and resentment; relieves depression
Feel like punishment	Feels soothing
Deplete energy	Generates energy
Lower self-value	Raises self-value
Impede compassion	Regulates guilt and shame
Require validation and absolution from others	Is self-rewarding and self-validating
Are likely to make the offended party feel that you just want to feel better	Is likely to make the offended party feel valued

You may have figured out that I've been talking in various ways about self-compassion in all the chapters of this book. Self-compassion is recognition of your basic humanity. It's a major component of your healing identity, rising directly from your core value. Self-compassion keeps the motivational system from getting hijacked by habituated defenses against vulnerability—namely withdrawal, resentment, and anger. Once you've been hurt by intimate betrayal, the path to core value must pass through self-compassion.

Self-compassion must always be in balance with compassion for loved ones. They really go together part and parcel, because it's nearly impossible to sustain one without the other. You simply cannot maintain self-compassion while consistently failing at compassion for loved ones, and you'll just burn out if you try to be compassionate to loved ones without sufficient self-compassion. The energy and strength required to consistently support the people you love has to be replenished by self-compassion. Think of it as the warnings that flight attendants give when demonstrating the proper use of the oxygen masks that drop in front of your face in the event of cabin decompression. If you're traveling with a small child, they warn, take care to put the mask on yourself before you try to put it on the child. They must tell you this, because your instinct is to put the mask on the kid first. But then you both pass out from oxygen deprivation. Self-compassion is just putting the oxygen mask on yourself first, which makes it possible to be compassionate to loved ones.

Note: While it is necessary to experience compassion for people you love, it is not necessary to interact with them, if the relationship is toxic and likely to produce more pain than good. Compassion heals you, even when it does not—or cannot—improve your relationship with the loved one.

EXERCISE

Make an honest and sincere effort to root out your hidden guilt and shame in the following exercise. If you're resentful, angry, anxious, obsessive, or depressed after intimate betrayal, you certainly have hidden guilt and shame that must be converted to self-compassion.

Copy the following lists on a sheet of paper, and fill them in, following the examples given.

Note: *Try to focus on what you are able to control, rather than how other people may respond to you. Personal effort, more than favorable responses from others, is the foundation of long-term well-being (Diener 2009). Moreover, focus on doing the best you can increases the likelihood of a favorable response from others, while preoccupation with getting a certain response from others will probably make them feel manipulated.*

Changing Guilt and Shame to Self-Compassion and Compassion for Loved Ones

Guilt and Shame	Apply Self-Compassion	Show Compassion
(Example: I wasn't there for the people I love in the months following my ex's betrayal.)	(Example: I was in pain, like millions before me who have endured intimate betrayal. I will make a dedicated effort to be there for loved ones in the future.)	(Example: I will set up an "appreciation" meeting or lunch with each loved one I have neglected.)
(Example: I insensitively hurt the feelings of a loved one when she said that she missed my ex.)	(Example: I was not in touch with my core value; I misinterpreted her feelings as another betrayal. I will be more discerning in the future.)	(Example: I will let her know that her feelings are important to me and that there is no excuse for what I said or for failing to consider her.)

(Example: I lied to my loved ones about the abuse I suffered in my marriage.)	(Example: I was so ashamed of it that I couldn't face the truth myself. I will embrace the truth in the future.)	(Example: I will assure my loved ones that they deserve the chance to be compassionate and helpful to me. I will be honest and open with them.)
(Example: I ignored calls from my estranged father when he reached out to me after my ex's betrayal.)	(Example: At that vulnerable time I couldn't let myself think about the long-term issues I have with my father.)	(Example: Although my father is a deeply flawed person, who was hurt early in his life, he has some caring and worthy qualities. I am not ready to resume a relationship with him, but I appreciate the gestures of love he has made.)

In filling out the lists, you probably felt a sense of empowerment in your ability to convert guilt and shame into self-compassion and compassion for loved ones. The more you practice this conversion, the easier it becomes.

Rational Guilt and Shame

Once again, most of the guilt and shame you experience about your betrayal are irrational artifacts of the early days of species evolution, when preserving attachment bonds was necessary for survival. But you will also have some rational guilt and shame about simple human mistakes you've made and a few personal failures of the sort that everyone occasionally commits in intimate relationships. These feelings will prevent healing and growth if ignored, explained away, or justified.

As with all emotions, guilt and shame lose their motivational power when we focus too much on how they feel and not enough on what they tell us to do. Focus on the feelings themselves, rather than acting on their motivations to connect, is likely to make you look for a quick fix to temporarily numb the pain (through blame, anger, or alcohol) or distract from it with compulsive behaviors (such as working all the time) or obsessions (thinking endlessly about something else). Quick fixes for guilt and shame typically lead to more failure and violation of values, which produce still more guilt and shame. Although you hear all the time from self-help sources that you should just "let go" of guilt and shame (and the resentment they cause), the fact is you *can't* let go of them for very long. They inevitably come back, usually before you know it. That's because attachment guilt and shame are motivations to connect to loved ones; they will persistently reemerge until you act on the motivation to connect. However, if all your love relationships are abusive or conflicted or simply will not support meaningful improvement, you can effectively substitute communal or spiritual connections to reduce guilt and shame and enhance core value.

EXERCISE: Rational Guilt

Divide a piece of paper into three columns. At the top of the first column write: "Things I regret doing or not doing." Then fill in the column with as many things as you can think of that you regret. (Note: Don't explain or justify the behavior you regret—that will only make you angrier and worsen the guilt and shame.)

At the top of the second column, write: "Self-compassion for the hurt or vulnerability I experienced before I did what I regret" and fill in that column. And at the top of the third column, write: "What I can do now to honor my values (and feel authentic)" and fill in that column as well.

Here's an example:

Things I regret doing or not doing	Self-compassion for the hurt or vulnerability I experienced before I did what I regret	What I can do now to honor my values (and feel authentic)
I regret that I ignored my wife and made her feel alone in our marriage. That did not justify her affair and desertion of our family, but my behavior was a violation of my core value.	I didn't know how to resolve the fear I felt about losing her whenever we could get close, and so I distanced myself from her. I will not make that mistake again.	I will make an effort to connect with significant people currently in my life; I will call my mother weekly, make sure that my children know that I am there for them, write a thank-you letter to friends who have supported me, strengthen my community connections, and renew my spiritual life.
I regret that I was critical and defensive in my marriage.	I felt criticized by others my whole life and had grown highly sensitive to feedback by the time I got married. I know that I can give and receive feedback from loved ones without being critical or defensive.	I will make an effort to stay connected when loved ones tell me something I don't like, understanding that we can reach resolution only if connected. I will make respectful behavior requests, making sure that we all agree that the requests are fair.

Read each row out loud. Hearing your voice utter the words will take much of the force out of the negative feelings and allow you to focus on their motivation to heal and improve. Reading aloud your regulation—how you will act on the motivation of guilt and shame to honor your deeper values—will reinforce the association of unpleasant feelings with the beneficial behaviors that relieve them.

The purpose of the above exercise is to build a habit of doing something to honor your deeper values whenever you experience guilt or shame. Okay, that's good advice, but guilt and shame are usually concealed by resentment or anger, so how are you supposed to know when they are present? The following exercise shows how to discover the guilt and shame that usually lurk beneath anger and resentment.

EXERCISE: Anger and Resentment Regulation

On a piece of paper, briefly describe an event in your recent past that triggered your anger or resentment. (Example: My ex-wife implied, yet again, that she left me for another man because I was a bad lover.) Then answer the following questions:

I'm angry, but what do I also feel guilty about? *(Example: I say the same kinds of things about her.)*

I'm resentful, but what do I also feel ashamed of? *(Example: I slip so easily into feeling inadequate as a lover during our marriage.)*

What will I do to improve, appreciate, connect, or protect? *(Example: In future relationships, I will open my heart to true intimacy. If problems arise—including sexual problems—I will address them with my partner, from my core value, in compassionate and respectful ways.)*

Hopefully you noticed in the above exercise that regulating the hidden guilt and shame that lurk beneath most anger and resentment empowers you to move forward in your journey toward healing and growth. (Failing to regulate hidden guilt and shame keeps you stuck on a treadmill of impotent resentment.) Healing, growth, and empowerment are inevitable when you act consistently from states of core value, but they do not always come quickly. Self-compassion will provide the patience necessary to bring about permanent change. When you eventually feel empowered—however long it takes—you will realize that most of the anger and resentment you experience now will have become completely unnecessary for safe, vibrant, and meaningful living.

Summary

Most of the guilt and shame following intimate betrayal are irrational, due more to ancient laws of attachment than to anything you did or any failures you perceived. Guilt and shame regarding love relationships always tell us to connect (love better), though not necessarily with the person who betrayed you. Self-compassion is the natural conduit to core value, healing, and growth.

CHAPTER 9

Overcoming Resentment and the Danger of Trust

This chapter describes the most persistent emotional state you're likely to experience after intimate betrayal. It shows how to break through the logjam of recurring resentment, which can make you feel that there's nothing you can do to make your life any better. The chapter ends with several beneficial replacements for the primary function of resentment after intimate betrayal: protection against the danger of trust.

Form and Function

Resentment is a derivative of innate anger, although it emerges later in childhood, as children develop a strong sense of fairness. Inherent in resentment is a perception of unfairness—you're not getting the help, appreciation, consideration, affection, reward, or praise you deserve.

Resentment shares the physiological characteristics of anger but is less intense and of longer duration; in other words, it occupies lower levels of arousal but lasts much, much longer. Where anger (when directed at others) is an aggressive exertion of power to get someone to back off or submit to what you want (either in reality or in your imagination), resentment is a defensive way of devaluing and mentally retaliating against those whom you perceive to be treating you unfairly.

Another difference between resentment and anger is that the latter is triggered by a specific stimulus—you insulted me (or I thought you did), so I got angry. The anger goes away soon after the stimulus attenuates—you apologize or I forget about it or choose to ignore it. In stark contrast, resentment is never specific and rarely goes away. It's a generalized defense against unfair relationships or environments, not just certain behaviors. Hence resentment persists despite changes in the behavior that may have stimulated it. Even if you apologize, I'll resent that you didn't do it sooner or that you weren't sincere or contrite enough, because I'm pretty sure you'll do it again in this unfair relationship or environment. Where anger is a tool to put out fires, resentment is more like a smoke alarm that's always on, just in case a spark should ignite. Other people might think your resentment is about the past and urge you to "let it go." But resentment is really about the future. After intimate betrayal, it seems to protect you from the danger of trusting again.

The Resentment Experience: More Than a Feeling

Describing what resentment feels like is difficult, because it builds mostly under the radar—by the time you know you're resentful, it's in a highly advanced stage. People often give vague descriptions such as "I'm in a sour mood," or "I'm just irritable." If you ask how they feel, they'll likely talk about other people cheating, lying, manipulating, or abusing them. At the same time, they will describe resentful others as having "a chip on their shoulders."

The experience of resentment is hard to pinpoint because it's really more of a mood than a discrete feeling. Emotions occur like waves that rise and fall, usually within a few minutes, while moods are like a steady current flowing beneath the surface of consciousness, always there, but rarely perceptible without careful self-reflection. This is an important distinction, because we tend to deal with resentment by trying to change how we feel, when the problem is the mood supporting the feelings. A change of feelings does little to alter moods. For example, if your underlying mood is positive, you are most likely feeling something like interest, enjoyment, compassion, or love. These emotions motivate behaviors that are caring, playful, romantic, supportive, cooperative, analytical, or creative. With this kind of behavioral reinforcement, a few negative feelings here and there, caused by disappointment, loss, or even transient thoughts of the betrayal, are not likely to change your mood. That's why, when you're in a good mood, things that might ordinarily hurt or offend you just roll off your back. But if your underlying mood is resentful, it's most likely causing visible waves of anger, anxiety, jealousy, or envy, which motivate behavior that is controlling, dominating, impulsive, possessive, confrontational, vindictive, dismissive, withdrawing, or rejecting. With this kind of behavioral reinforcement, a few positive feelings here and there will do little to alter your mood. For these reasons, "sorting through your feelings" (commonly suggested by self-help sources) will not relieve resentment for very long. But replacing its defensive function with more viable, growth-oriented protections, like those described in this chapter, will make resentment and the self-harm it causes mere relics of the past.

Resentment as Distrust

Resentment has a strong component of self-punishment. Though usually obscured by the inclination to devalue those we resent, the punitive nature of resentment is revealed in sentiments such as:

"Why did I ever trust her?"

"I knew he'd let me down!"

"How could I have been stupid enough to believe him again?"

The false appeal of self-punishment is that it seems to keep us safe from future hurt and disappointment. If you get mad enough at yourself—and punish yourself sufficiently—you might not be "so stupid" as to trust or rely on that person—or someone like him—again. This illusion of protection from hurt is the "great lie" of resentment. In fact, you get hurt a lot more often when you're resentful, for the simple reason that people react to what they see. And resentment *looks* very different on the outside from the way it *feels* on the inside. To appreciate this important point about resentment, try the following "mirror test."

Sometime when you're alone, look in a mirror for at least thirty seconds before you begin the test. (We tend to pose in the mirror rather than look candidly at it. But it's difficult to hold a pose for more than thirty seconds.) Begin the test by thinking about the unfairness of your betrayal. As you do, you will notice your heart rate increase slightly, your neck tighten, and your shoulders and jaw stiffen. You will probably look down and away from the mirror as you think about the unfairness of the way you were treated. But try to hold onto those thoughts and force yourself to look back at the mirror. When you do, you'll see what the world sees. On the inside you feel abused, victimized, hurt, and vulnerable. On the outside, you look unfriendly at best, or at worst, a little mean-spirited. The look of resentment completely belies your internal experience. It is likely to prompt negative reactions from others, through no fault of yours. If you feel that other people just don't understand you, resentment is probably not allowing the real you to show.

Chains of Resentment

Nobody resents just one thing. Things you resent tend to interlock with each other like the links of a chain. Resentment about your partner's dishonesty will link onto resentment about his messiness or her compulsion for neatness, which in turn links onto resentment of his lateness, her carelessness, his "obsession with sex," or her "sexual coldness"—whatever you regard as unfair. Relationships that suffer betrayal typically feature a chain of resentment extending back many years before the betrayal. (I've never seen a case where both partners felt like the burdens and rewards of the relationship were fairly distributed prior to the betrayal.) Once the betrayal occurs, the chain of resentment is likely to take on a self-linking life of its own; that is, the partners begin to look for things to resent. The logic seems to be that hurt and disappointment are less likely to blindside them as long as they carry around all that they have suffered, as constant reminders to be vigilant.

As resentments link onto each other to form a long chain, it becomes difficult to tell trivial matters from serious ones—when you pick up a chain by one link, you hold the weight of the entire chain. Thus minor matters can seem to carry the same weight as vitally important ones. This confusion causes the kind of overreactions described in the section on high emotional reactivity in Chapter 1. A long chain of resentment underlies most angry outbursts.

Chains of resentment impair concentration, diminish fine motor skills, and lower overall performance competence. You won't work as well or drive your vehicle as safely if you're chronically resentful.

The Health Risk

You may have read about medical studies showing that anger has many dangerous effects on health. The consensus description is the "heart-attack emotion" and the "not-so-silent killer." The headlines usually don't tell you that it's not just any anger that does the damage; it's a specific kind of "hostile" anger that lasts for an extended period of time. Hostile anger has a retaliation motive—you fantasize about putting someone down or paying her back for a perceived injury. Most anger—such as that triggered by abrupt noises, ordinary irritations, frustrations, or unpleasant events—is not hostile. The damage to your health is done not by ordinary anger but by resentment, with its built-in retaliation impulse. (When resentful, you think often of how you've been wronged and how the offender should be devalued.) The other factor that makes anger so harmful to health is its duration. Anger that lasts longer than a few minutes does more health damage than frequent anger or intense anger. Once again, the culprit is not simply anger, which gives way in fairly short order to exhaustion. It's resentment, which can go on for days, weeks, or even years.

Resentment is likely to keep your blood pressure at a higher level than is normal for you. Chronic resentment may eventually damage the blood vessels in your heart and brain. It constricts the nerve endings in your muscles. This constriction can cause chronic, low-grade muscle and back pain. Long-lasting resentment can cause:

- destruction of T cells, lowering the immune system (If you're resentful you probably have lots of little aches and pains and get frequent colds, bouts of flu, headaches, muscle aches, stomachaches, or gastrointestinal problems.)

- hypertension, which increases the threat of stroke and heart attack

- heart disease

- cancer

- addictions

- depression

- shortened life span

The chronicity of resentment consumes enormous amounts of energy that would normally go into something you're interested in or enjoy. As you begin to adopt the core value defenses described below, you will almost certainly have more interest and enjoyment in your life.

The Core Value Defenses

Fortunately, there are far healthier and more functional protections from future hurt than resentment. The following candidates rise directly from states of core value:

- self-compassion

- compassion for loved ones

- compassionate assertiveness

- self-forgiveness

- conviction

Self-Compassion

After intimate betrayal, the surest path to core value is through self-compassion, as described in the last chapter. Self-compassion is incompatible with resentment in that it focuses on healing rather than devaluing. However, it's not as forceful as resentment, which has the energizing effects of the hormones epinephrine and cortisol. These make you feel more powerful, but only for a while. Ironically, resentment persists because of the hormonally driven illusion that we need it to feel safe, when quite the opposite is true. To feel safe, we need self-compassion, which helps us recognize our basic humanity, resilience, and strengths, and to focus on healing, improving, and growth.

Dislodge Resentment with Self-Compassion

Due to the hormonal reinforcements of resentment, it will take determined effort and practice to replace it with self-compassion as the primary defense against future hurt. The purpose of the exercise below is twofold. First, it is meant to condition a core value response to occur automatically when resentful thoughts occur. Second, it should replace the powerlessness of resentment with a sense of empowerment to make your life better.

To begin your practice, make an exhaustive list of everything—large and small, serious and trivial—that you resent about your betrayer. This will include everything from his lying to you (or abusing you or cheating on you or stealing from you) to his leaving dirty dishes in the sink or dropping his clothes next to the hamper. (It's necessary to include trivial items on your list because the weight of the chain of resentment makes them seem overly important; when a chain of resentment is active, nothing is too petty to resent.) After you compile your exhaustive list, recite it into a digital recorder and play it back. The added objectivity the recitation will bring should prompt you to cross off the lesser items that aren't so bad when isolated from the other links on the chain of resentment. You will be left with the more serious items, which you can process with the following exercise.

Note: If you wish to repair the relationship with your betrayer, most of the items you process below will require negotiation. In Part IV, I'll add a negotiation step to this exercise.

EXERCISE IN PROTECTIVE SELF-COMPASSION

On a piece of paper, list as many things as you can think of that you resent about your partner. (Example: She did not want to go to couples counseling to deal with our problems before the affair.) Leave space for writing in between each item on the list.

Then, under each item, describe how you will access your core value. (Example: I will invoke my core value bank; focus on building value and appreciation into my everyday life; learn; exercise; take care of my health; connect to those I love; forgive and learn from my mistakes; and make familial, communal, or spiritual connections.)

Read your resentments—along with your strategies for restoring core value—aloud. You cannot spend too much effort associating hurt and vulnerability with behaviors motivated by your core value, so that any occurrence of the former will automatically invoke the later. The result, eventually, will be an automatic reflex to improve, appreciate, protect, or connect whenever you feel hurt.

How Compassion for Self and Others Protects You

Compassion is simply the best psychological defense you can have, far superior to the most common alternatives: resentment, withdrawal, distraction, or aggression. Genuine compassion prevents future hurt by:

- restoring core value, which lowers the ability of other people to make you feel inadequate or unlovable

- rarely stimulating anger in others, thus making hostile or destructive defenses less necessary

- offering superior protection from the pain of betrayed trust

Compassion never condones or excuses bad behavior. In fact, it's not about behavior at all. Compassion means "to suffer with." It focuses on the pain and human frailty that make people behave badly, while recognizing that the continuation of bad or irresponsible behavior will hurt them more. For example, the worst thing you can do for an abusive person is to excuse or tolerate the abuse, because doing so would lead to self-loathing from continual violation of his deepest values. Neither is it compassionate to allow children to behave irresponsibly, lest they painfully learn how cruel the world is to the irresponsible.

No one has been hurt due to compassion, though a great many people have been harmed as a result of unwise trust. Compassion reduces the likelihood of unwise trust, as it provides deeper understanding of the danger presented by those unable to regulate their hurt without hurting others.

My primary example of compassion's protection from unwise trust comes from a far more extreme place than even intimate betrayal. Many years ago, I began an anger-regulation group with prisoners convicted of multiple murders. (My hypothesis—that teaching violent criminals to develop a sense of core value through self-compassion and compassion for others would reduce crime—didn't exactly set the state government afire with support. They wouldn't let us test it on anyone but those who would never again be free.) Already serving consecutive life terms, these hapless prisoners had no incentive to refrain from violence against other prisoners. As one of them put it, "So they give me another life sentence; I'll get out in the twenty-third century instead of the twenty-fourth."

Multiple murderers tend to be in the system for a long time, usually from early childhood. Their case files look like small mattresses. As I read page after page of social service reports documenting the terrible things that happened to these men when they were innocent children, I couldn't help but develop a deep compassion for their inestimable suffering. To my surprise, compassion helped me understand that the level of hurt these men had suffered was too great. The treatment helped them do well in the confines of prison (the training significantly reduced their violence), but in the high-stress, complex world outside, with its anxiety-provoking choices and emotional demands, they were likely to revert to their primary form of self-empowerment: harming others.

Compassion reveals who you can trust by allowing you to look more deeply into people's hearts to see how they empower themselves against hurt and vulnerability—by building and creating or by harming and destroying, by honoring their deeper values or by deceit, infidelity, or abuse.

Compassionate Assertiveness

Compassionate assertiveness is standing up for your values, rights, and preferences in ways that honor the values, rights, and preferences of others. The quintessential balance of self-compassion with compassion for others, compassionate assertiveness allays much of the fear of compassion that naturally follows intimate betrayal—fear that you'll be manipulated or taken advantage of, or that you'll set yourself up for more betrayal.

While it will not prevent betrayal in future relationships, compassionate assertiveness will lower the baseline resentment that so often justifies deceitful behavior in the mind of the betrayer. In other words, it will make betrayal harder to perpetrate.

Tilda came to see me after her husband, Martin, had cheated on her. Once she completed the foundational recovery work—building a "healing identity" and using self-compassion as a stimulus to enact core value behaviors—she was ready to practice compassionate assertiveness. We used a dispute with Martin, which had begun many years before his affair. Tilda had always believed he was too critical of their children, especially their son. Their history was to fight about it in a classic parental standoff, with Martin convinced that Tilda was too permissive, while Tilda was sure that Martin was too strict. I've used a paraphrase of Tilda's responses as examples in the exercise below.

EXERCISE: Compassionate Assertiveness

Note: The purpose of using events that occurred before the betrayal is not to stir regret and certainly not to assign blame. The intention is to build hope for a better future by replacing the defensive function of resentment with compassionate assertiveness.

On a separate piece of paper, describe something you resent about the partner who betrayed you—preferably a pattern of behavior that began before the betrayal. (Example: He constantly criticized our children and eroded their self-esteem.)

Then, describe how you might have handled the incident with compassionate assertiveness. (Example: I could have told my partner that I know he loves our children very much and wants what is best for them; it's just that so much criticism is harmful to them and ineffective as discipline—they keep acting out. I could have suggested we discipline them in ways that support their social and educational development.)

Repeat this practice with several different examples of things you resent and ways you could have handled those things with compassionate assertiveness.

Notice that in her exercise, Tilda honored Martin's deeper values, giving herself the best chance of getting him to see her perspective. Had the couple been able to practice compassionate assertiveness, their dispute would have become a negotiation about simple behavior choices, rather than a recurring, resentment-breeding power struggle about whose preferences would prevail. Without compassionate assertiveness, each partner heard the other saying "You're a bad parent," a scolding that would drown out any parenting "facts" they might bring to the argument.

If Tilda and Martin had practiced compassionate assertiveness, a red flag of potential betrayal would have been revealed before it wreaked so much damage on their relationship. Martin was especially critical of his son, who reminded him a great deal of himself, in that they shared many of the same personality traits, including stubbornness and impulsivity. (We tend to be highly intolerant of loved ones who display qualities or behaviors we don't like in ourselves.) Instead of regulating his vulnerability through a core value behavior, such as strengthening his relationship with his son and helping him manage impulsiveness, Martin chose to criticize and devalue him. Of course, this approach made both father and son feel more inadequate and unlovable. It also raised the likelihood that Martin would seek some kind of adrenaline escape, such as an affair. Where resentful standoffs mask the vulnerabilities that can lead to betrayal, compassionate assertiveness reveals them before they damage the relationship.

Doing the Compassionate Assertiveness Exercise above on pre-betrayal disputes is a gateway to using the skill in present and future relationships. The formula is simple: honor the values, rights, and preferences of others while asserting your own, and they are more likely to honor yours. Of course, compassionate assertiveness won't guarantee you a positive response, but you will always strengthen your core value when you try. And you will also make it more difficult for others to respond negatively to you.

Self-Forgiveness

You're probably thinking, "Why do I have to forgive myself? *He* betrayed *me!*" Unfair though it may seem, you have to forgive yourself in order to:

- overcome the anger and self-recrimination of resentment

- increase self-value, which will automatically motivate behavior in your long-term best interests

- provide a more effective defense against hurt (You're stronger when you forgive yourself than when you punish yourself.)

The next obvious question is "What am I forgiving myself for? What did I do?" This one's a little trickier. You didn't *do* anything to forgive. It's just that betrayal cuts us off from core value and makes us feel inadequate or unlovable. Self-forgiveness gives back the power to determine our well-being by invoking core value and the desire to heal, improve, and grow. Odd though it might sound, forgiving yourself for feeling inadequate and unlovable makes you adequate and lovable. Try the following exercise to see if it works that way for you.

SELF-FORGIVENESS EXERCISE: Take Back Your Power

Copy the following "I forgive" … "I know" statement onto a sheet of paper. For each of eight items from the exhaustive resentment list you made above, supply a resentment/self-value pair demonstrating self-forgiveness. Example:

I forgive myself for losing sight of my core value and feeling inadequate or unlovable when my partner... (Item 1 resent-

ment: rejected my wish to go to couples counseling before the betrayal).

I know that I'm loving and lovable because I'm caring and compassionate. I show my care and compassion by... (Item 1 self-value: going to counseling on my own.)

Now read your self-forgiveness declarations out loud, and feel the power in your voice. Repeating this exercise with everything on your resentment list will condition self-forgiveness to occur each time you start to feel resentful in the future.

Conviction

Conviction is the strong belief that a behavior is right, moral, and consistent with your deeper values. Like resentment, conviction provides a sense of certainty about what we believe and do. The difference is that the relative certainty of conviction is likely to endure in all moods and frames of mind, whereas self-doubt returns as soon as the intensity of resentment fades.

The best way to know that you're acting out of conviction and not resentment is to state *why* your behavior is right, moral, and consistent with your deeper values. If your answer has conviction, it will represent your deeper values. If it is resentful, it will devalue someone else. For example, Terry knew that he was right to take the children and leave his alcoholic wife, who was harming them emotionally. He continued to regard her compassionately and support her as well as he could, but he had to put the well-being of their children first.

However, the path to conviction was not easy for Terry, who dragged a long chain of resentment into his first day of treatment. It was clear from the first fifteen minutes of talking to him that he was bound in what I call a "pendulum of pain." Resentment would pull him away from his wife, until the distance between them grew to the critical point of actual separation. Then, like clockwork, the shame of his perceived failure as a husband and guilt over what would happen to his wife if he left swung him back toward her. This constant pendulum swing between nearly leaving on the one end and not quite reconnecting on the other had gone on for nearly seven years before I met him. What finally gave him the strength to take the kids and leave was his hard work to develop core value and conviction in treatment. As it turned out, his bold action prompted his wife to seek professional help for her drinking. After a few relapses—typical in addiction treatment—she was able to maintain sobriety, and the family was reunited.

When you act with conviction, you might be disappointed or saddened by the outcome of specific behaviors or negotiations, but you'll be far less likely to regret your behavior, as you almost always do when you act resentfully. Terry would have felt sad if his wife had not overcome her drinking problem after he left, but he would not have regretted leaving to protect their children. On the other hand, had he left out of resentment, he would have devalued his wife, which would have made the separation harder on his children, in addition to reinforcing his maladaptive defenses. In other words, he would have been filled with negative emotion that would eventually turn to regret.

"For" vs. "Against"

An important feature of conviction is that it's *for* something—such as the well-being of loved ones, justice, fair treatment, or equality—while resentment is *against* something—mistreatment of loved ones, injustice, or unfairness. The distinction may seem subtle, but it's crucial to healing and growth. Those who hate injustice want retribution and triumph, not fairness. They fantasize about punishment of their unjust opponents, who stir "justifiable" contempt. If Terry had left his wife out of resentment, he most likely would have developed contempt for her, and covered up his guilt with fantasies of punishment: "She got what she deserved!" This would have harmed their children and alienated him from his core value.

Being *for* something creates positive feelings of interest, passion, or joy, which tend to improve health and relationships. Being *against* something foments negative feelings of anger, contempt, envy, or disgust, which have deleterious effects on health and relationships.

EXERCISE: Conviction

The purpose of this exercise is to develop a habit of acting with conviction in all matters important to you. Although it uses past decisions and behaviors, the point is less about compensating for past mistakes than acting with conviction now and in the future.

> **On a separate piece of paper, describe a decision you made or something you did after your betrayal that has been troublesome to you.** *(Example: I decided to have no contact with my in-laws.)*

> **State why your decision was right, moral, and consistent with your deeper values.** *(Example: My in-laws are naturally biased toward their son and unfairly lobby me to take him back when I know that the relationship is harmful to both of us. In time, when they accept my decision, I may reestablish connection with them.)*

Read what you wrote aloud to reinforce your sense of conviction.

Under the extreme stress of betrayal, we're all apt to violate our deeper values to some degree. It's likely that you made some decisions after the betrayal that you do not believe were right, moral, or consistent with your deeper values. For those incidents, use the exercise below to develop your sense of conviction.

> **Describe a decision you made or something you did after your betrayal that you now clearly regret.** *(Example: I decided to have no contact with my in-laws.)*

State why your decision was not right, moral, or consistent with your deeper values, and what corrective actions you might take. *(Example: I was very hurt and acted on my retaliation impulse to hurt my ex by rejecting his parents. My in-laws were innocent victims, and I will no longer deny them access to their grandchildren.)*

Conviction reduces hidden guilt and shame by helping us align behavior with deeper values.

If you're unable to correct your actions, use the exercises in Chapter 8 on converting guilt and shame into self-compassion. Guilt and shame keep you locked in the past, while self-compassion invokes your core value in the present. Conviction based on your deeper values is focused on the present and future: "I am now doing what I deeply believe is the right thing, because it honors my deeper values in the following way..." and "I *will* do what I deeply believe is the right thing!"

Conviction and Trust

When you're true to your deeper values, whatever they may be, it's easier to tell when other people are true to theirs. For example, if you value intimacy, you will understand that it requires expressions of vulnerability and weakness as well as strength and resilience. It requires a balance of compassion with self-compassion. It thrives on self-enhancement through occasional selflessness. With conviction, you'll do these things because they feel right to you, not to get your partner to love you or do something for you. With conviction, you'll be sincere, with little chance of seeming manipulative—that is, doing something merely to get something. Then you can better discern whether your partner is behaving out of conviction or out of manipulation, or merely attempting to avoid feeling manipulated. In short, you'll gain a better sense of whom to trust. Though not foolproof, conviction tends to breed conviction and expose untrustworthiness.

The following exercise contrasts conviction with resentment as protections from future hurt.

EXERCISE: Conviction as Protection

The following exercise contrasts conviction with resentment as protections from future hurt.

On a piece of paper, briefly describe something you resent. *(Example: My self-centered ex-husband took advantage of my trust and compassion with his constant lies and manipulation.)*

Explain how the resentment you described above protects you from the danger of trust. *(Example: I know that I can't trust any man who seems nice and caring in the beginning.)*

Explain how conviction can protect you in the future. *(Example: When I am true to my values, it's easier to see when other people are true to theirs. I will trust myself to be the best person and partner I can be. Even if I'm disappointed, I will know that I did the best I could.)*

You may have noticed, as you described the protective function of resentment, that it greatly limits growth and value creation. And when you described conviction, you promoted growth, through focus on your deeper values.

Repeat the above exercise, with all the things you resent, until you consistently feel the strength of conviction, relative to the powerlessness of resentment. It may take a while; the betrayal has made you focus too much on how other people behave, when your true power is within you. With practice, you will see that conviction feels more genuine than resentment and is far more likely to bring healing and growth.

Summary

Resentment is more of a persistent mood than an emotion. It tends to dominate the emotional landscape after intimate betrayal because it seems to protect against the danger of trusting again. But it offers a mere illusion of safety, as you're likely to get hurt more often when resentful. In terms of health, healing, and growth, the costs of resentment are enormous. Much better alternatives are the "core value defenses": self-compassion, compassion for loved ones, compassionate assertiveness, self-forgiveness, and conviction. These defenses strengthen your core value, enhance your sense of self, and raise the likelihood of making good judgments about whom to trust in the future.

Continued core value work will help eliminate resentment and unwise trust from your life and thereby improve all your relationships. It will also prepare you to love again, which is the topic of Part III.

Part III

Loving Again

I have tried to show in previous chapters that attachment pain in general—and the severe pain of intimate betrayal in particular—did not evolve in our species to harm or punish us. Rather, they developed to motivate more emotional investment in love relationships (of all kinds) and in communal or spiritual connections, each of which offered survival advantages. Part III addresses the major concerns of loving again: trusting wisely, avoiding potential betrayers, and longing for intimacy. Although the section discusses these challenges in the context of new relationships, please read it—and do the exercises —even if you choose to repair the relationship with your betrayer. The issues involved in that choice will be taken up in Part IV, but this section will be an excellent preparation.

CHAPTER 10

The Path to Wise Trust

Human beings need to trust. Trust allays anxiety, helps lift depression, and makes it possible to consistently invest interest and enjoyment in one another. There could be no civilization, enduring health, or mental wellness without trust. The most ordinary interpersonal, commercial, medical, and legal interactions would be impossible without some degree of trust. Distrust is fraught with anxiety and resentment. No loneliness is lonelier than distrust.

As you are painfully aware, intimate betrayal impairs the ability to trust. That wouldn't be so bad if trust-inhibitions affected only love relationships, as it would give you time to heal before attempting to form new intimate bonds. But impairments in the ability to trust have a way of spilling into all relationships, including those with children. This chapter will help remove those impairments by showing you the path to wise trust.

First, let's distinguish wise trust from its opposites: blind trust and suspiciousness.

Blind trust puts faith in someone without regard to demonstrated reliability or trustworthiness. It's more a reluctance to experience the doubt, anxiety, and loneliness of distrust than an endorsement of the other person's better qualities. *Suspiciousness* is focused on the mere possibility of betrayal. *Wise trust* assesses the *probability* of betrayal, in recognition that we are all frail creatures capable of betrayal in weaker moments. Realistically, it's possible that any of us could betray a loved one. Blind trust denies this darker characteristic of human nature; suspiciousness exaggerates it. Wise trust is an assessment that the probability of betrayal is low.

Trusting wisely in close relationships is a slow and gradual process. It has to be; any accurate assessment of the probability of betrayal must be based on the demonstration of reliability over time and under stress. Unfortunately, there's a loose cannon in assessing the probability of anything at all. In elevated levels, anxiety presents a major barrier to wise trust.

Anxiety

In small doses, anxiety is a vital emotion. Without it, you could be killed crossing the street and would find yourself largely ill-prepared for the important tasks of life. Anxiety tells you to pay attention, because something different might happen. Simple anxiety is activated by actual or anticipated change in the environment or in your imagination. It makes you focus on dealing with the pending change by shutting out most other information. The anxiety about a fire in the room gets you to stop thinking about what you'll have for lunch so you can focus on putting out the fire.

Anxiety becomes a problem when it taps into an underlying sense of incompetence that makes it feel like you don't know what to do or what to focus on. The aroused but indecisive brain begins to scan, taking in a lot more surface information a lot more rapidly, with less discernment of what is relevant. In other words, your thoughts race, sometimes like a runaway freight train.

Because scanning takes in a lot of superficial information, assessments based on it have a higher likelihood of error, which is why our judgments while anxious are often wrong. What's more, the scanning process itself raises anxiety with its flurry of possibilities, most of which are unrelated to the change that triggered the anxiety in the first place. The more you scan, the more anxious you get. You may have noticed this with your children. If you yell at them for making mistakes, you can pretty much bet that they'll keep making the same ones over and over. Yelling at a child to be careful after he's dropped a glass, for instance, makes him unconsciously associate anxiety with picking up the glass. Instead of focusing on how to pick it up safely, his brain begins to scan as soon as he gets near the glass. He pays less attention to what he's doing and more to the thoughts racing through his mind, increasing the likelihood of dropping the glass. If you want to decrease the likelihood of broken glasses, lower his anxiety by softly and calmly suggesting how to pick up a glass—for example, "Be sure when you pick up the glass that you feel the coolness in the palm of your hand." Focus, the opposite of scanning, lowers anxiety. Anxiety regulation—a necessity for trusting wisely—requires focus.

Anxiety Regulation

A good way to gain focus while anxious is to give your racing thoughts answers. This will slow down the scanning of unlikely possibilities and allow focus on the more likely ones. Practicing the exercise below can help develop a habit of answering anxious thoughts.

Write down some of the thoughts that race through your mind when you're anxious. Then record your answers to them, following the examples below.

My Racing Thoughts	My Answers
(Example: I'll screw things up.)	(Example: I'll try my best to avoid mistakes and to correct any I might make.)
(Example: My friends will abandon me.)	(Example: If my friends are displeased, I'll explain my intentions sincerely and honestly.)
(Example: My children will hate me.)	(Example: I'll let them know how much I care about them. If they display negative feelings, I'll let them know that they can safely express their feelings to me.)
(Example: No one will love me.)	(Example: I will try to see other people's perspectives and be more compassionate. My compassion will make me feel more lovable.)
(Example: I'll hate dating again.)	(Example: I'll give myself time, and when I'm ready, I'll try to find something to like about dating, such as meeting new people or getting to know them better.)
(Example: My work team will lose the contract.)	(Example: We'll work hard to keep that from happening, but if it does, we'll learn from it and do better the next time.)

The exercise above should be repeated until answers to your anxious thoughts become automatic.

Some of your anxious thoughts, of course, require more than an answer. For those you need to develop contingency plans. For the purpose of regulating anxiety, a contingency plan consists of simple thoughts about what you will do if the worst actually happens—in other words, if "A" happens, I will do "B."

The lists below are an extension of the lists above. In the left column, record any thoughts that continue to stir anxiety after you give them an "answer." In the right column, briefly describe your contingency plans.

My Anxious Thoughts	My Contingency Plans
(Example: I'm worried about my finances since my abusive husband left.)	(Example: I will go online to find as much free advice on financial planning as I can. I will research ways to earn money from home.)
(Example: Since the betrayal, I have fallen behind in my projects at work, and I worry that my boss will lose patience with me.)	(Example: I will prioritize my focus on the major steps of each project. I will persist in my efforts. I'll try to find something in the project that I might enjoy or take an interest in. I will let my boss know how much I appreciate her patience.)

(Example: I worry about my weight, as I keep overeating since the betrayal.)	(Example: I will run through the boxes of my core value bank before eating, to help me stay focused on eating for health. I will eat slowly, putting the fork down after each bite to chew my food well. I will try to walk thirty minutes a day to help normalize my appetite.)
(Example: I worry if I will ever again be able to trust.)	(Example: I will focus on self-compassion and be patient with myself. I will focus on compassion for other people, which will help me see how well they self-regulate and whether they are worthy of trust. I will act on my deeper values and accept any disappointment that may result.)

If you have trouble with any of the contingency plans you attempted to write down, try to bring out more detail in the plan. For example, regarding finances after betrayal (a very common worry), you could write down the points that you want to make when e-mailing a financial advisor or when interviewing for a job. Other possibilities: research optimal resume construction and targeting, use job search tools, find an employment agency, and so on. In general, more detailed plans result in less anxiety.

The Probability of Betrayed Trust

Anxiety is about possibility; wise trust is about probability. It is possible that *anyone* can betray us; the trick is figuring out the *likelihood* of betrayal.

Intimate betrayal most often occurs when partners violate their deeper values to gain a temporary sense of empowerment. The way that potential partners empower themselves when feeling vulnerable is the most important clue in assessing the probability of betrayal. Knowing facts about their historical behavior in intimate relationships helps, of course. But that is not always possible. Fortunately, there are subtle signals that can help assess probability. The potential partner who becomes angry, resentful, or depressed when feeling vulnerable is more likely to shut down or punish (withdraw interest or reject) or control (demand certain behaviors) or seek some kind of temporary ego boost through infidelity or deceit. In contrast, the potential partner who responds to the prospect of vulnerability by trying to improve the situation, appreciate, protect, or connect is far less likely to betray you.

Use this practice to assess the probability that a betrayal of trust will occur in a current relationship: On a piece of paper, write the sentence "When feeling vulnerable (anxious, devalued, rejected, powerless, inadequate, unlovable), my partner is likely to..." Then, in one column, list as many of these words as you think apply: improve, appreciate, protect, connect. And in a second column, list as many of these words as you think apply: shut down, get angry, deceive, cheat, abuse substances, abuse me. If the relationship is new, do this exercise every couple of weeks, until you learn more about the prospective partner.

If you decide that the likelihood of betrayal is not low, insist that the prospective partner learn self-regulation skills, either from this book or in skill-based therapy. (Considerable self-regulation help is available at compassionpower.com.) She must learn how to behave in ways that will make her feel empowered without hurting or betraying you.

When Disappointment Feels like Betrayal

Another way that anxiety poses as distrust is in elevated sensitivity to possible hurt. Anxiety after intimate betrayal greatly amplifies sensitivity to hurt, sometimes to the point where disappointment feels like betrayal.

Many of my divorced clients begin treatment feeling anxious, depressed, and completely unable to trust the people closest to them. Nevertheless, they seem convinced that the mere passage of time has healed the wounds of their past betrayals. Their presenting complaints are mostly about disappointments in their current relationships—intimate and otherwise—that explode with the emotional intensity of betrayal. Here are a few examples:

- Phil broke up with his new girlfriend (his second serious relationship after his ex betrayed him) because she was uncomfortable going to church with him, even though she told him from the start that she wasn't religious.

- Keisha fought with her new husband because he noticed other women in the grocery store, though he knew that her ex had been unfaithful to her.

- Tyrone left his new wife because she was "skeptical about everything" he said to her, although he admitted that she was not emotionally abusive like his ex.

- Shocked and appalled when her elderly mother forgot her birthday, Elizabeth broke off all contact, just before her mother's untimely death.

- Geneen had lost all her former friends because she believed they weren't "available" to her whenever she needed them after her ex's betrayal.

It's easy to say that these folks simply have not recovered from intimate betrayals of the past, and of course that's true. But there's a particular reason for the constant distrust in their current relationships. They misinterpret the anxiety signals that occur with—or immediately before—feelings of disappointment. Instead of interpreting their sudden rise in anxiety as a mere signal of imminent change, they view the anxiety, though relatively minor, as a sign of disaster. The resulting surge of adrenaline amplifies the disappointment and makes the situation seem like trust-destroying betrayal.

Most of my clients, including all those mentioned above, learn early in treatment that disappointment is part of ordinary living and not at all the same as betrayal. Disappointment is inevitable in relationships. As frail human beings subject to forgetfulness, occasional insensitivity, and absorption in our own defenses against hurt, we are bound to disappoint each other. I like to put it this way: disappointment is about the way the house looks at a given moment; betrayal is a gaping crack in the foundation. We cannot assume that displaced furniture signals a crack in the foundation, just as we cannot improve the foundation by rearranging the furniture. Some disappointments can be dealt with by negotiation, correction, or compromise; others must be accepted and tolerated, if the relationship is otherwise viable and important to you. In contrast, betrayal is nonnegotiable, intolerable, and unacceptable without significant relationship repair.

The list below is a guide for keeping disappointment—which is really about frustrated preferences—distinct from betrayal, so that one never feels like the other.

We trust loved ones to:

- not intentionally hurt us

- maintain the security of the relationship through interest, compassion, trust, and love

- accept and value us for who we are

- keep our best interests at heart (in balance with the best interests of other family members)

- respect us

- support us in times of need

- care about our pain, discomfort, vulnerability, and distress, and offer to help

- want us to be happy

We prefer that loved ones:

- never hurt us, even unintentionally

- not show (or feel) interest in or attraction to anyone else

- share all our values, tastes, and preferences

- put our interests first

- idealize us and never hint of displeasure or disappointment

- think—and say often—that we're smart, attractive, talented, successful, and so on

- regulate our negative emotions—in other words, eliminate our pain, vulnerability, and discomfort

- make us happy

Preferences may well be important to you, or even be deal-breakers for certain relationships. Just know that preferences are subject to disappointment (and subject to reciprocation, meaning that you're unlikely to get more than you give). Disappointment is inevitable in human relationships; betrayal should never occur. We have to keep them distinct if we hope to achieve any kind of satisfaction in close relationships.

Disappointment and Negotiation

You can match any two people on the planet—even identical twins—and they will have conflicts of preferences that have to be negotiated, if they want a close relationship with each other. To maintain viable relationships, we must be able to negotiate when disappointed, which means regulating any anxiety that is misinterpreted as betrayal. We have to be able to say to ourselves and to our loved ones at the outset of negotiation, "I'm disappointed, but I'm okay." If we can feel this and show it to loved ones, negotiation is about simple behavior choices that pose no threat to trust, compassion, or love.

Realistically, it will take several weeks of the core value work described in Chapters 5 and 6, and then a few repetitions of the exercise below to reach the point where disappointment never feels like betrayal.

EXERCISE: Disappointment vs. Betrayal

On a separate sheet of paper, copy the following questions and fill in your answers. Repeat the exercise with as many interactions as you can recall that felt like betrayal.

Describe something your partner did recently that upset you. (Example: My new boyfriend ogled an attractive woman in the grocery store, the day after I confided *to him that my ex-husband cheated on me throughout our marriage.)*

Do you think it was a violation of trust? *(Yes.)*

What else *might* **it have been? What was your partner's perspective of it?** *(Example: I read a report that men are more susceptible to visual stimulation and that sometimes they're not immediately aware of where their eyes go. That's exactly how he described it.)*

Access your core value and then describe what you can do to negotiate behavior change. *(Example: When I'm in touch with my core value, I can say, "I know it's not that big a deal for you to glance at other women and that sometimes you might not know that you do it. But if you could try to be more mindful about it when you're with me, I would really appreciate it.")*

Notice in the example above that the negotiation did not allege betrayal; it expressed a sincere preference. This kind of expression improves the chances of a positive outcome, by giving the other person an opportunity to act compassionately rather than defensively. More important, you have a better chance of feeling authentic in expressing your preferences through compassionate assertiveness, compared to making demands, which your partner will likely regard as "controlling."

Self-Compassion Means Slow Trust

Continuing to do core value work and the exercises in this book will help you trust wisely. But please don't let the natural desire to trust people you care for rush what is a necessarily slow process. Think of it this way: the more slowly that trust returns, the better; slow trust is more likely to have a solid and durable foundation. Be patient with yourself. Your trusting nature is not lost; it's just a little bruised. Those who love you will probably understand what you've been through and will most likely be patient with you. If they are worthy of your trust, they have an intuitive understanding of this: three of the four positive attachment emotions—interest, compassion, and love—are unconditional in healthy relationships. But the fourth—trust—must be earned.

The next chapter tackles one of the scariest things about loving again: the possibility of meeting another betrayer.

Summary

Human beings need to trust, but we need to trust wisely. Blind trust ignores the possibilities of betrayal. Suspiciousness exaggerates them. Wise trust assesses the probability of future betrayal. Trusting wisely is a slow process; accurate assessment of the probability of betrayal has to be based on the demonstration of reliability over time and under stress. The loose cannon in trusting wisely is anxiety, which must be regulated to have successful relationships. Otherwise, we are apt to perceive betrayal in the unavoidable disappointments of potentially good relationships. Self-compassion, patience, and much core value work will put you well on the path to wise trust.

CHAPTER 11

How to Know If You're Dating a Future Betrayer

The first big test on the path to wise trust comes in dating. My heartfelt reason for including this brief chapter comes from so many stories of hurt clients who rushed into dating, only to be betrayed yet again. It can happen to anyone. In general, the people most likely to betray intimate bonds are quite skilled at pretending to be everything you've always wanted in a partner. They can be so seductive that you are unlikely to notice the red flags of future betrayal—deceitful, angry, controlling, possessive, jealous, overly flirtatious, or violent behavior—until you're already attached and feeling protective.

Because the red flags of betrayal tend to show themselves too late, a more useful guide for dating is what I call the "very early warning signs" of a potentially high-risk relationship—signs that are often visible before an attachment bond is formed. The following is a list of qualities to look for in a potential lover. Like all early warning signs, they do not constitute conclusive evidence that someone will betray you. They are intended merely as a roadmap for staying safe in love.

During the early stages of dating, your partner probably won't do any of the following to you directly. But you may be able to notice a few of the identified attitudes and behaviors played out toward others. You should also be able to recognize some of them retrospectively in the partner who betrayed you.

Very Early Warning Sign #1: Blaming

Avoid anyone who blames his negative feelings and failures on someone else. You have to be really careful here; blamers can seduce by making you look great in comparison to previous partners:

"You're so smart, sensitive, caring, and loving—not like the jerks I usually meet."

"You've shown me all the things that love should be, just when I thought that only cheats and liars dated anymore."

"You're so calm and together; he was so crazy and paranoid."

"You're so sweet and honest, you would never betray me like she did."

"Why couldn't I have met you before I got involved with that self-centered jerk?"

Hearing how wonderful you are compared to your predecessors might make you think that all your date really needs is the understanding and love of a good partner to change a run of "bad luck." It's nice to be kind and refrain from judging others, but don't ignore the "law of blame": eventually, it flows to the closest person. When you become the closest person, the blamer's blame will surely turn on you.

Blamers usually suffer from victim identity. They will be sure to point out in dating that, like you, they have been betrayed in previous relationships. If you're lucky, they'll be a little more conspicuous by mentioning unfaithful spouses who drove them to cheat, or vindictive lovers who couldn't forgive the most "minor" mistakes, or greedy ex-partners who stole their money and then sued them for more. As long as they identify with being victims, they will justify any retaliation they enact or compensation they take. A blamer, if you come to love one, will eventually perceive injury from you and retaliate with some form of betrayal.

Very Early Warning Sign #2: Resentment

Resentful people, as we saw in Chapter 9, feel like they are not getting the help, consideration, praise, reward, or affection they think is due them. They get so caught up in their "rights" and locked into their own perspectives that they become insensitive to the rights and perspectives of others. Of course the resentment will not be directed toward you at first, but you will most likely see it in their references to others. If you come to love a resentful person, you'll eventually bear the brunt of that resentment and almost certainly feel diminished in the relationship. Eventually, you'll feel betrayed.

Very Early Warning Sign #3: Entitlement

People with a sense of entitlement feel that they deserve special consideration and special treatment. They may cut in front of others waiting in line, smoke wherever they want, drive any way they want, say anything they like, and do pretty much whatever they choose, with little consideration of others.

Driven by high expectations of what other people should do for them, they feel offended when the world doesn't cooperate. (And the world won't cooperate with entitlement needs, once they're over five years old and not so cute anymore.) So it seems only fair, from their myopic perspectives, that they get some kind of compensation for their constant frustrations. Typical rationalizations include:

"It's so hard being me, I shouldn't have to wait in line, too!"

"With all I have to put up with, I deserve to take a few supplies from the office."

"With the kind of day I had, how could they expect me to listen to their problems?"

"All the taxes I pay, and they bother me about this little deduction!"

"The way I hit the golf ball today, I should get the best seat in the restaurant!"

"She just flat out refused to cook my dinner, so she got what she deserved."

"He said he loved me, but he hardly ever bought me things. No wonder I was attracted to someone else."

During the glow of infatuation, the entitled person will regard you as equally entitled to special consideration from others. He'll "support" you to take all you can from "unfair" others. But after the glow wears off, his feelings, preferences, and desires will clearly be more important than yours. If you agree with that, you'll get depressed. If you disagree, you'll get betrayed.

Very Early Warning Sign #4: Superiority

Potential betrayers tend to have hierarchical self-esteem; that is, they need to feel better than others to feel okay about themselves. They constantly point out ways in which they are smarter, more sensitive, or more talented than others. This behavior can be seductive in dating, as she'll insist that you, too, are superior. (You must be to merit her company.) But the hierarchy will become clear over time, with you on the bottom.

The most abusive form of hierarchical self-esteem is predatory self-esteem. To feel good about themselves, those with predatory self-esteem need to make other people feel bad about themselves. People who disagree with them or fail to recognize their talents are "stupid," "ignorant," or "narrow-minded." Many will score high on self-esteem tests if they come for treatment (usually under court order), while everyone else in their family tests low. But once intervention increases the self-esteem of the emotionally beaten-down spouses and children, who then no longer internalize the put-downs as a consequence of their "inferiority," the self-esteem of predators plummets. They simply can't feel good when they can't make others feel bad.

A variation on this very early warning sign is self-righteousness. People who disagree with the self-righteous are worse than "wrong": they're "immoral"! Those who don't keep house a certain way have no idea how "decent" people should live. If you don't meet their whims, you're selfish and unlovable.

Very Early Warning Sign #5: Sarcasm

Sarcasm comes in many forms. Sometimes it's just poorly timed humor—saying the wrong thing in the wrong context. Sometimes it's innocently insensitive, with no intention to hurt or offend. More often, it's hostile and meant to devalue. The purpose is to undermine someone or to shake her confidence, either for a temporary ego gain or for some strategic advantage.

Sarcastic people tend to be heavy into impression management, often trying too hard to sound smart or witty. In dating, their sarcasm will be directed at others. In a relationship, it will center on you. If you are hurt by their sarcasm, they will criticize you for having a "poor sense of humor." They'll feel misunderstood and unappreciated most of the time. In their minds, those feelings will justify whatever betrayal they choose to enact.

Very Early Warning Sign #6: Minor Jealousy

Minor jealousy is more subtle than the obvious red flag of controlling and possessive behavior. It looks more like this: Your date is slightly uncomfortable when you talk to—or even look at—someone you might possibly be attracted to. Nothing will be said, but the uncomfortable feeling is apparent.

The tough thing about minor jealousy in dating is that you actually want a tiny bit of it, to know that the other person cares. (You wouldn't want to love someone who couldn't care less if you slept with the entire volleyball team.) But a little bit of jealousy goes a long, long way. Think of it as a drop of powerfully concentrated liquid in a huge bucket of water. More than a tiny drop will poison any relationship you might develop and, more important, put you in harm's way. Jealousy, even in mild forms, is a potent predictor of future betrayal.

Very Early Warning Sign #7: Rushing

I have had many women clients complain that their new boyfriends don't try very hard to pursue them or to sweep them off their feet. I always say, "How lucky you are!"

Those who go "too fast" (defined as whatever makes you uncomfortable) do not respect personal boundaries. (One way to define "abuse" is "behavior that violates personal boundaries.") The rusher will often promise, at least implicitly, to meet all your desires and preferences, a promise impossible to keep. A telltale sign is his offering a bit more than you think you deserve in the early stages of the relationship. It is not flattering to have someone want you so much that she doesn't care whether you're comfortable with her desires and intentions. Make sure that anyone you date shows respect for your comfort level. A lover insensitive to your internal world will likely betray you.

Very Early Warning Sign #8: Childlike Playfulness and Affection

Few characteristics are more seductive than playfulness and child-like expressions of affection. A playful lover can revitalize your emotions and reawaken a sense of sheer joy. But, as with most good things, there's a downside.

People who play with toddler-like innocence tend to be toddler-like in other ways as well. They are likely to use the toddler defenses of blame, denial, and avoidance, rendering the most minor relationship negotiation impossible. You're likely to witness subtle hints of impatience, entitlement, envy, and temper tantrums in their dealings with others. These will increase in frequency and intensity as your relationship progresses. You might enjoy the playfulness and affection in a potential lover, but be sure not to overlook it as an early warning sign of potential betrayal.

Trust in Yourself

While prudent concern in dating is a good thing, you want to be sure that your caution is proactive, rather than reactive; you want it based on trust of your perceptions and instincts, rather than distrust of love and relationships. The ability to trust yourself rises from your core value. As long as you stay attuned to it, you will naturally gravitate toward those who truly value you as a person, and become less susceptible to seduction by potential betrayers.

Yet even when you're firmly grounded in your core value, it's possible to be unaware of hidden resentment, anger, deceit, jealousy, or abusive tendencies in the people you date. That's because it's easy for those prone to such tendencies to put on a "dating face." They have a more fluid sense of self than most people, so it's easier to pour it into any container they think you might like.

But they can't—and won't—stay in a nice or loving container once you establish a close relationship. Their resentment, anger, deceit, or abuse will lead eventually to some form of betrayal.

Below is a checklist to help you keep track of the number of times the very early warning signs show themselves in your dates.

Very Early Warning Signs Checklist

Identify how many times, on your last three dates or visits, you witnessed your partner do the following to you or to someone else:

_____ blame

_____ show resentment

_____ display a sense of entitlement or expect special consideration

_____ act superior

_____ be sarcastic

_____ show minor (or any kind of) jealousy

_____ rush you for more contact or intimacy or commitment

_____ suddenly withdraw playfulness and affection to pout or get angry

_____ **Total incidents of the early warning signs**

By way of comparison, identify how many times, on your early dates or visits, you witnessed your ex-partner, who eventually betrayed you, do the following to you or to others:

_____ blame

_____ show resentment

_____ display a sense of entitlement or expect special consideration

_____ act superior

_____ be sarcastic

_____ show minor (or any kind of) jealousy

_____ rush you for more contact or intimacy or commitment

_____ suddenly withdraw playfulness and affection to pout or get angry

_____ **Total incidents of the early warning signs**

Of course, you want the total number of incidents to be as low as possible. Anything higher than "two" is cause for alarm. You deserve better.

The next chapter, "Intimacy and the Hungry Heart," will focus on getting better.

Summary

The people most likely to betray intimate trust are skilled at manipulation and making themselves seem to be what you want. Yet they are apt to show at least one of the very early warning signs at the beginning of relationships: blame, resentment, entitlement, superiority, sarcasm, minor jealousy, a tendency to "rush" you, or childlike playfulness and affection. The very early warning signs are a useful guide to establishing safe relationships in the future.

CHAPTER 12

Intimacy and the Hungry Heart

During the long recovery from intimate betrayal, a bruised heart is likely to grow hungry for intimate contact. It may weaken from that hunger, but it will never starve to death. Sooner or later, the hungry hearts of most betrayed people kick through any remaining defensive walls to feed on love. The previous chapters of this book were dedicated to nurturing the bruised heart from within, so it doesn't try to love out of desperation. This chapter will guide you through the maze of what can be the most rewarding and frightening of human endeavors: intimate connection.

Human beings come into the world with a drive for intimate contact. But if the most important attachment relationships provide more punishment than reward, as in intimate betrayal, the drive to love is constrained by fear and shame. Eventually the recovering heart, though hungry for intimacy, is likely to feed on the only emotional experience forceful enough to break through inhibitions of fear and shame: passion.

Intimacy vs. Passion

Passion is the fast food of love, immediately gratifying and filled with calories but with little of the nutritional value of true intimacy. In terms of relationship function, passion *brings* us together, but intimacy *keeps* us together; passion moves us, but intimacy makes us grow. Hence they dominate different stages of relationships, with intimacy becoming prominent as passion wanes. This fact is hardly surprising. The nuance of intimacy—truly knowing another person—can scarcely emerge in the thrall of passion. When emotions run high, partners tend to project their feelings onto each other: "If I feel this, you must feel it too." Their mutual projection creates an illusion that they are somehow merged. I call it the *illusion of sameness*.

Intimacy vs. the Illusion of Sameness

The biggest mistake we make in regard to intimate connection is assuming that our partners' experience is the same as ours and that the events we experience and the behaviors we enact mean the same to them as they do to us. This singular illusion is largely a product of the hormone that mediates the formation of emotional bonds. Oxytocin causes feelings of closeness, warmth, and trust, as it facilitates idealized projections. The illusion of sameness allows us to create some measure of safety in the face of the vulnerability that intimate connections evoke. To ward off feelings of inadequacy and fear of rejection, we talk ourselves into pleasant delusions:

"Our hearts beat as one."

"We're soul mates."

"We're so close that we complete each other's sentences."

"She really believes in me."

160

"He really *gets* me."

The price of any safety and security the illusion of sameness may offer is an inability to see our partners apart from our feelings about them. Partners who want to feel like "soul mates" will begin to feel invisible, unheard, criticized, controlled, and betrayed when they try to express their individuality. Most fights in relationships afflicted with the illusion of sameness can be reduced to the demand "You must be more like me, and see the world the way I do!"

No "Me-Harmony"

Lovers who suffer the illusion of sameness inevitably discover that their partners are not simply copies of themselves. Your partner almost certainly has a different temperament, different experiences, different hormones or hormonal levels, a different trajectory of emotional development, and different support networks, all of which will cause him to give different emotional meanings to events and experiences. If you do not appreciate and respect those differences, you will feel betrayed by them.

To love freely in the highly complex and emotionally demanding modern world, we must respect all our differences, appreciate many of them, and tolerate those we cannot appreciate. The great beauty of harmony in relationships, as in music, lies in combinations of different notes, not endlessly repeated unison.

Intimacy and Discovery

True intimacy regulates the urge to project feelings onto your partner by replacing it with appreciation of your *separateness:* "You add dimensions to my experience *because* you're different from me." The more you are able to love your partner because of your differences, the more dimensions of self you gain. In a continual process of discovery, you come to know your lover, while learning about yourself from the way you behave in the context of love. That's why you can't really know yourself until you love another person, and you can't completely know other people without loving them.

Intimate discovery is not primarily factual; love is not profiling. It's almost an entirely emotional sense of *how* we experience the world, rather than an intellectual understanding of *what* we experience. More than just learning that you like sunsets, intimacy is understanding what sunsets mean to you.

The discovery process of intimacy yields a kind of *binocular vision*—the ability to see the world through your partner's eyes, knowing her desires, dreams, ambitions, vulnerabilities, and strengths, while simultaneously understanding your own. You cannot grasp the reality of an intimate relationship by seeing the world through just one lens—yours or your partner's. The complete reality of the relationship emerges only by looking through two separate lenses simultaneously.

Early Messages of Intimacy

Almost from the beginning, relationships give off subtle messages about the level of intimacy they are likely to support. These are conveyed in nonverbal cues—body language, tone of voice, facial expression, tension, relaxation, focus, distractedness, silence, hesitation, impatience, discomfort, eagerness, or enthusiasm. They encourage or discourage self-disclosure and individuality. They promise or constrain growth and support. They ease the ability to reveal anything about the true self, or they limit discussions to the "social" or "dating" self. It's hard to pinpoint a specific meaning of any one of these gestures, but in accumulation, they create a sense of how much intimacy the relationship will offer.

The following checklist can help make the subtle messages about future intimacy more explicit. You can use it to gauge the potential of any newly developing relationship. By way of comparison, use it to measure the early stages of the relationship that betrayed you.

Intimacy Checklist

___ Can you disclose anything about yourself to your partner, including your deepest thoughts and feelings, without fear of rejection or misunderstanding? Does your partner feel safe in disclosing anything to you?

___ Is the overall message of your relationship "grow, expand, create, disclose, reveal"? Or is it, "hide, conceal, think only in certain ways, behave only in certain ways, feel only certain things"?

___ Do you feel that you can both develop into the best people you can be as the relationship progresses?

___ Does your partner fully accept that you have thoughts, beliefs, preferences, and feelings that differ from his? Can he respect those differences and accept them without trying to change them?

___ Do you want to accept that your partner has thoughts, beliefs, preferences, and feelings that differ from yours? Can you respect those differences and accept them without trying to change them?

___ What are your primary dreams and ambitions? Does your partner understand and accept them? What are your partner's dreams and ambitions? Do you truly understand and accept them?

After you go through the checklist, ask your partner to go through it as well, and discuss your answers. Doing so should reveal just how intimate your relationship is likely to become. If you're both lucky and willing to work, you can achieve an *advanced intimate connection,* in which both partners:

- accept one another for who they are

- experience high regard for each other

- protect the welfare of one another

- are "there" for each other, to give emotional support during difficult times

- share occasional interest, excitement, enjoyment, and joy, as well as sadness, loss, and disappointment

- communicate freely on more than practical or superficial levels

The Opposite of Intimacy: Emotional Need

Even after a lot of care and core value work, a heart hungry for intimacy may occasionally cry out its longing in anxiety or despair. When that happens, we should not confuse the perfectly natural yearning for a close relationship with an emotional need for one. The best chance of finding freely given love in a safe relationship is to approach it out of desire, not emotional need.

"Freedom to love" is a key phrase. To be free to do something, we must be free not to do it. We are free to love only to the extent that we aren't forced into it in vain attempts to relieve guilt, shame, or fear of abandonment, or by misguided efforts to make up for past mistakes, or, worst of all, by misinterpreting vulnerable feelings as signals of emotional need.

An emotional need is a preference or desire that you've decided must be gratified to maintain equilibrium; that is, you can't be well or feel whole without it.

The perception of need begins with a rise in emotional intensity—you feel more strongly about doing this or having that. As the intensity increases, it can feel like you "need" to do or have it, for one compelling reason: it's the same emotional process as biological need. When emotion suddenly rises, your brain confuses preferences and desires with biological needs.

Here's how it works: You don't normally feel anything about breathing, until you have difficulty doing it. At that point, emotional intensity spikes to signal an imminent survival threat. Similarly, you normally don't feel anything when your partner is working on his computer. But if you speak to him, and he seems to ignore you, your emotional intensity is likely to increase until the desire for his attention seems to be a need for it. Instead of trying to engage your partner's interest because you desire it, you'll demand it, because you "need" it, or punish him for failing to meet your needs. Now which do you think is more likely to get you the kind of attention you most desire from a loved one, showing interest in him or demanding that he "meet your needs?"

The habit of interpreting preferences and desires as needs vastly oversimplifies subjective experience. Emotional intensity can rise and fall for a great many reasons, most of which have little psychological meaning. For instance, your current physiological state (hungry, thirsty, tired, bloated, sick, agitated, hormonal, and so on), as well as the time of day, sudden changes in weather, and the current state of your core value, influence variations in emotional intensity to a greater extent than most preferences or desires. If you're starving, exhausted, sick, freezing, or depressed, how loving, appreciative, communicative, safe, or secure can you feel?

Even though the association is largely artificial and accidental, when the increase in emotional intensity stimulates a perception of need, that perception, in turn, increases emotional intensity. In other words, the perception of need becomes self-reinforcing: "I feel it, therefore I need it, and if I need it, I have to feel it more."

This self-perpetuating feature of the perception of need is predominantly unconscious. The way it gathers conscious strength is by falsely explaining negative experience. For example, if I perceive myself to have emotional needs, and I feel bad in any way for any reason, it's because my needs aren't being met. It doesn't matter that I'm tired, not exercising, bored, ineffective at work, or stressed from the commute or the declining stock market, or, most important, whether I'm mistreating you or otherwise violating my deeper values; the reason I feel bad is that you're not meeting my needs.

Once the brain becomes convinced that it needs something, pursuit of it can easily become obsessive, compulsive, or addictive. In terms of *motivation*, perceived emotional needs are quite similar to addictions. My clients who think they have strong emotional needs almost always begin treatment with descriptions of their relationships that sound a lot more like addiction than desire:

"I can't live without her."

"I shake all over when he's gone."

"It's like heaven when he's nice to me."

One client actually said, "She's my drug. I can't face the day without a dose of her."

While the body contributes on a cellular level to *addiction*, the mind exclusively decides that we have an emotional need. The feeling can become so powerful that it makes us believe we have holes within us that someone else must fill. That's a tragic—and false—assumption that almost always leads to bad relationships. No one has holes within, only drives to create value.

Big Holes Attract Small Cups

If you believe you have holes within, you will almost certainly attract a partner with a small cup to fill them. Here's why.

For one thing, people with big cups—that is, people who have a lot of love to give—don't look for partners with big holes. They want partners who also have big cups, who can give as much as they get in a relationship. But if I perceive myself to have a small cup, or not much to give, I'll be attracted to someone who thinks she has big holes, because her "emotional needs" will inspire me to become her rescuer or hero or whatever idealization she projects. Of course, I won't be able to uphold the role of giver or rescuer for very long, because it's so unnatural for me and my small cup. Eventually I'll condemn her for the very "needs" that first attracted me: "Nobody could meet your needs; you're insatiable!"

When "I Love You" Degenerates into "Meet My Needs!"

No matter how seductive "I need you" may sound in popular songs, the partner who "needs" you cannot freely love you. Most of the painful conflicts of intimate relationships begin with one partner making an emotional request—motivated by a perceived "need"—that the other, motivated by a different "need," regards as a demand. This is the classic demand-withdrawal dynamic mentioned in Chapter 8: The more one partner demands, the less the other can give; the more one pleads, the farther away the other retreats. Both feel like victims. Indeed, any disagreement can feel like abuse when the perceived "need" of one to be validated crashes headlong into the "need" of the other not to feel manipulated:

> "If you loved me," one partner argues, "you'd do what I want"
> (or "you'd see the world the way I do").

"If you loved me, you wouldn't try to control me," the other counters.

"If you loved me, you would do this."

"If you loved me, you wouldn't ask me to do that."

As long as you perceive yourself to have emotional needs that your partner must gratify, your desire to love is reduced to "getting your needs met," which your partner takes to mean that he has to give up who he is to meet your needs."

Become the Partner You Most Want to Be

So how do you get what you want in intimate relationships? Think of Gandhi's famous quote about being the change you wish to see in the world. Due to the relationship dynamics known as *positive reciprocity* and *negative reactivity* (Margolin and Christensen 1981), people in intimate relationships tend to respond in kind to positive and negative actions by their partners, especially under stress. Caring usually prompts caring:

"I feel bad that you're hurt."

"I feel bad that you're hurt too."

Anger tends to create power struggles:

"You have to do what I want."

"No, you have to do what I want!"

And resentment breeds resentment:

"I don't care about your feelings, but you *must* care about my feelings."

"Well I don't care about your feelings either, because you don't care about my feelings."

If you want a positive response, your best bet is to act positively, that is, from your core value. But there's a more important reason to be the partner you most want to be.

Research has taught us that your best chance of being happy in an intimate relationship is to be happy before it starts. The data suggest that there is a set point of happiness, to which we tend to revert following positive and negative life experiences (Brickman, Coates, and Janoff-Bulman 1978). People can suffer great loss, even crippling accidents or disease, and within a couple of years, rise to their level of happiness from before their misfortune. Similarly, joyous events, such as getting married, winning a lottery, or getting a great job, have a positive effect only for a year or so, before we revert to our original set points of happiness.

You can change your set point for happiness, but the change has to come from within, not from marriage, lotteries, or success at work. Your best chance of finding a partner you can be happy with is to be happy on your own. And the key to that happiness is to live according to your deepest values.

In the relationship surveys we use at CompassionPower, we ask people what kind of partners they would like to have and what kind of partners they would like to be. In general, people want to be loving, compassionate, supportive, and sexy. They want their partners to be those things too. But they also want them to be generous, flexible, and fair.

Most of the people in our surveys did not report that they wanted to be generous, flexible, and fair themselves, but they definitely wanted those qualities in their partners. It's not that the respondents wanted to be stingy, rigid, or unfair; it just didn't occur to them to list those qualities for themselves. That's understandable, considering that, in general, we're much better at judging others than assessing ourselves. We tend to be hypersensitive when someone is unfair, ungenerous, or inflexible toward us, but we really have to stop and reflect—if not go on a weekend retreat—to even come close to an adequate evaluation of whether we are those things to others.

Like it or not, we have to develop the self-awareness to know when we're being the partners we most want to be. But it's worth the effort; it's really the only chance of finding a safe intimate relationship.

The exercise below asks you to specify what you're looking for in an intimate partner. Knowing what you want will go a long way toward reducing the anxiety inherent in safely loving again after intimate betrayal. It will also highlight the best route to becoming the partner you most want to be.

EXERCISE: What I Want in a Partner

On a sheet of paper, list and describe the qualities you would like in a partner. Follow the example below, but list the specific traits and behaviors that are important to you.

I want my partner to be:

loving—to express affection, engage in conversation, rub my back

compassionate—to care about how I feel, offer help or comfort, make an effort to sympathize with me

supportive—to notice when I need help or comfort, help me to think through problems, encourage me to do my best without criticism or lecturing

sexy—to desire me, find me attractive, touch me the way I like, look deeply into my eyes *generous—to give freely of time, energy, spirit, and available resources*

flexible—to never make up his mind before we discuss it, be willing to entertain different perspectives, accept my influence

fair—to objectively consider whether a behavior or a request is just and reasonable and ask my input about its fairness

THE PARTNER I WANT TO BECOME

Your best chance of getting the partner you most want to have is to be the partner you most want to be. And your best chance of getting what you want is to give it. So next, list those same qualities again, and after each one, describe what you can do to give your partner the same things you want to receive.

Chances are, you wrote many of the same things on both lists. If you use these lists as a guide for giving what you want to receive, you will feel more successful, but not because your partner is certain to respond in kind. Although you'll greatly increase the odds of a reciprocal response, it's never guaranteed. What is guaranteed is the inherent reward of doing what you believe is right.

Teach Me How to Love You

The worst thing you can do when starting a new relationship is believe that you know how to make intimate unions work.

In reality, there's no way that any of us *could* know. Biology, which takes many, many generations to change, has not prepared us for love's special challenges in our rapidly changing culture. Tradition is hopelessly outdated—the old socialized roles and norms have broken down almost completely—and pop psychology gives little more than platitudes or oversimplified and contradictory advice.

But don't despair; the human brain is amazingly adaptive and capable of learning. The only thing that blocks us from being able to learn how to love better is the ego; we simply don't want to admit that we don't know how to do it right. To be relieved of the awful burden of ego, repeat the following out loud, three times:

> "I don't know what the hell I'm doing when it comes to making a modern intimate relationship work!"

Once relieved of the burden of defending our egotistical preconceptions and prejudices about how relationships *should* be—and how our partners should see the world—we are free to apply our intelligence and creativity to learning how to love the unique people we come to love. The most loving thing you can say to your partner is "Teach me how to love you, and I will teach you how to love me." Learning how to love your partner, while teaching your partner how to love you, will surpass any kind of marriage therapy or self-help materials you might access.

The following exercises, "Teach Me How to Love You" and "This Is How to Love Me," should give you an idea of the behaviors that will work for the unique couple that you and your partner comprise. While there's no question that intimate relationships require work to be successful, the last thing we want to do is make it hard for our partners to love us. In fact, we want to make it as easy as we can. Thus the exercises instruct you to tell your partner what will make it easier for you to do what he wants you to do for him to feel loved. They also prompt you to ask your partner what will make it easier for him to do what you want him to do for you to feel loved.

EXERCISE: Teach Me How to Love You

Ask your partner, "What can I do to make you feel loved?" Write down your partner's response. (Example: "Surprise me now and then with flowers.")

Assuming that your partner responds with something you can do, tell her what will make it easier for you to do that. (Example: "Tell me you are pleased with the flowers when I bring them."

EXERCISE: This Is How to Love Me

On a sheet of paper, write out the following statements and questions and fill in the answers.

I feel loved when you... (Example: greet me when I come home.)

I will make it easier for you to do this by... (Example: showing appreciation when you do it and doing the same for you.)

Is there something else I can do to make it easier for you? (Write your partner's response.)

Repeat the series of questions multiple times in order to come up with several things your partner can do, and several ways for you to make those things easier.

Communicating with your partner about the content of the above exercises will go a long way toward establishing a safe and satisfying intimate relationship. Love looks a little different with each couple. How to do it well is a lesson you must teach each other.

The next part of the book, Part IV, is for those readers who want to repair a betrayed relationship. If you're one of them but don't feel quite ready to do it, just give yourself time. Keep doing core value work, and don't attempt repair until you feel ready. If you are not interested in repairing the relationship with your betrayer, skip to the epilogue.

Summary

The desire for intimacy often creates a hungry heart following intimate betrayal. Safe love is that which is given freely, from desire, rather than in response to perceived emotional need. It requires sensitivity to, appreciation of, and respect for your differences, with minimal attempts to get your partner to be more like you. The chances of finding a safe intimate connection increase with a willingness to forego preconceptions of how love should be, in order to learn how to love the unique person you come to love. The mantra of successful relationships in modern times is "Teach me how to love you, and I will teach you how to love me."

Part IV

Rebuilding a Betrayed Relationship

It goes without saying that the path to repairing a relationship that has suffered betrayal is strewn with pitfalls, not the least of which are heightened anxiety and self-doubt. This section of the book will guide you through the major barriers to repairing a betrayed relationship. First, it will help you decide whether you truly want to repair, as it is very easy to mistake a feeling that you *should* repair with a genuine desire for renewed bonds. It will present formal agreements between you and your partner that will help facilitate the repair process. It will then describe the reconnection dilemma that follows intimate betrayal, help you decide which level of reconnection you want to achieve, and guide you toward achieving it.

CHAPTER 13

Rebuilding a Relationship with Your Betrayer

Why does this section come near the end of a book on healing and growth? It's not because relationship repair following intimate betrayal is so bloody difficult, although that is certainly true. The repair section had to come near the end because focus on repair too soon would distract from the more important task of personal healing. Repairing a relationship damaged by betrayal activates the natural defenses against trusting someone who has hurt you. Those defenses are designed to help you ward off future hurt, but they work against healing past hurt; they prevent you from building the value into your life that ultimately heals and encourages growth. As you may have discovered by now, it takes a great deal of healing to accept emotionally what you probably understood intellectually: *you* are not damaged, but your relationship has been damaged.

Only when you are well on your way toward personal healing can you meaningfully evaluate the extent of the damage done to your relationship and whether you truly want to repair it.

But no matter how much healing you achieve, turning your focus to repair will likely provoke torrents of self-doubt, as automatic defenses spring back into place. Doubts emerge in the form of anxiety or dread, perhaps alternating with optimism about the possibilities of repair. These nagging questions will likely come up again and again:

"Why am I doing this?"

"Am I a fool?"

"Am I setting myself up to be hurt again?"

Doubts about repair are a natural response to having been hurt. They do not necessarily mean that the choice to repair is unwise or wrong for you. They are not stop signs; they are caution signals that you must heed.

Doubts about repair can actually benefit both you and your partner by slowing down the repair process. The more slowly that repair progresses, the more likely it is to endure. As in building a house, haste and corner-cutting in relationship repair can be disastrous. Each attempt to repair that fails further fragments hope and lowers the odds of eventual success. So don't suppress your doubts; *encourage* them. If your decision to attempt repair is rooted in your core value, it will survive all tests of doubt.

Though it may sound counterintuitive, you can use self-doubt therapeutically. You can deliberately use it to rewire your brain in favor of repair, by giving each doubt an answer from your core value, much the way you did in the chapter on anxiety.

Begin by asking yourself, "Why do I want to repair this relationship?" Be brutally honest with yourself, and write down your responses. The following example includes questions to consider.

Why I Want to Repair My Relationship

1. Love

    a. How much do I love this person?

    b. Is the bond between us a strong one or maintained by habit, convenience, or coercion?

2. Well-being of our children

    a. How would it benefit our children if their parents stayed together?

    b. How might it harm them if their parents stayed together?

    c. How would it benefit them if their parents separated?

    d. How might it harm them if their parents separated?

3. Finances

    a. What is the financial advantage of repair?

    b. What is the financial advantage of termination?

4. Family and support network

    a. How do my family and friends feel about repair?

    b. How important (to me) are their feelings about repair?

5. Shared history

    a. How would repairing our relationship honor our shared history?

    b. How might separation honor our shared history?

6. Respect

    a. Is my partner a fundamentally good and loving person?

Read your responses out loud. That should give you a bit more objectivity to decide if you truly want to repair.

If you truly want to repair—or still aren't sure—use your responses above to answer the recurring questions:

"Why am I doing this?"

"Am I a fool?"

"Am I setting myself up to be hurt again?"

Answer each question from your core value, following the example below. (If you need to, take a couple of minutes to run through your core value bank before answering.)

Why am I doing this (choosing to repair)? (Example: My love for my partner is important to me, the well-being of my children is better served if we stay together, financial security is assured if we stay together, connections with my in-laws are important to me, my marriage vows are important to me, our shared history is important to me, my partner is a fundamentally good and lovable person.)

Am I being a fool? (Example: I'm never a fool when I act on my core value. But I will be smart about the repair process.)

Am I setting myself up to be hurt again? (Example: No, because I'm doing what I think is right. Any hurt I experience will be sadness and disappointment, but I will know that I am worthy of love, affection, interest, trust, and compassion, because I am able to give those things. If I don't feel able to give those things, I will practice more self-compassion and core value work until I am ready.)

Answering doubts from your core value each time they occur builds conviction about repair and will provide a sense of authenticity to your ultimate decision.

Become Clear on What You Want

To enhance your sense of authentic conviction, it's best to become clear in your own mind about what you want from your partner before you try to convey what he has to do to repair. That's no easy task, as a lot of contradictory impulses are involved, such as retaliation and punishment on the one hand and a deep desire for peace and reconciliation on the other. Unfortunately, research offers little help in suggesting what your partner should do to repair the damage wrought by betrayal; what seems to work for many people doesn't work at all for many others. There is no empirically supported formula for what you "should want" or what your partner "should do" to repair your relationship.

I have found two points to be crucial in working with thousands of clients who want to repair betrayed relationships. First, you must look deep within your heart to decide what you want from your partner. There will be contradictory impulses, but those are usually more superficial and can be resolved on the level of core value—what is most important and most meaningful to you. Second, your partner should make every effort to comply with whatever you decide you want him to do to repair your relationship. He must understand that compassion isn't giving what he wants to give; compassion is giving what will help you reinvest in a loving relationship.

While you won't be able to trust your partner for some time, you can and must trust yourself to know what is best for you and what will help you feel safe during and after the repair process. To help gain that clarity, write out your answers to the very difficult questions below. It's crucial that you try to imagine what it would be like if your partner did what you want and, as a consequence, how your behavior would change.

Be utterly honest in your responses.

WHAT I WANT FROM MY PARTNER

Do I want my partner to grasp the full extent of my hurt?

If so, what will my partner's full understanding of my hurt do for me?

If my partner grasps the full extent of my hurt, I will be more (check all that apply):

___ *loving*

___ *affectionate*

___ *compassionate*

___ *flexible*

___ *fair*

___ *generous*

___ *other (describe)*

Do I want my partner to answer detailed questions about the betrayal?

If so, what are the questions I would like answered?

If my partner fully and honestly answers all my questions I will be more (check all that apply):

___ *loving*

___ *affectionate*

___ compassionate

___ flexible

___ fair

___ generous

___ other (describe)

Do I want atonement or penance from my partner?

If so, what kind of atonement or penance would I like?

What form would it take?

If my partner performs the acts of atonement or penance I have described, I will be more (check all that apply):

___ loving

___ affectionate

___ compassionate

___ flexible

___ fair

___ generous

___ other (describe)

Do I want my partner to suffer as I have suffered?

If so, what will her suffering do for me?

If my partner suffers as I have suffered, I will be more (check all that apply):

___ loving

__ *affectionate*

__ *compassionate*

__ *flexible*

__ *fair*

__ *generous*

__ *other (describe)*

You may have noticed in filling out the list above that even if your partner does what you want and feels the way you want, it will make little or no difference in your behavior. If that is the case, you probably are not ready to repair your relationship. Give more attention to personal healing—self-compassion and core value work—before you attempt relationship repair.

If your partner doing what you want would change your behavior, there is another step you should take before sharing what you've written. It would be wise to become clear on what your partner cannot do, must not do, and must do to repair your relationship.

What Your Partner Cannot Do:

- heal you (This entire book is dedicated to helping you heal yourself.)

- make you trust her (She must be trustworthy, but your trust must come from your own healing and will probably take a long time.)

- resolve your resentment (He should give you no cause for future resentment, but you must resolve your past resentment, once it has become part of your internal defense system, as discussed in Chapter 9.)

What Your Partner Must Not Do:

- ask you to heal him

- ask you to trust or forgive her (Such a request indicates a lack of understanding of the healing process and puts unfair pressure on you to compensate for her mistakes.)

- tell you to "get over it" or "stop living in the past" (This kind of command indicates a lack of sufficient compassion.)

What Your Partner Must Do:

- value and appreciate you—show that you're an important part of his life

- respect you as an equal—listen to you, without trying to control you or dismiss your opinions

- regulate her guilt, shame, anxiety, resentment, and anger, without blaming them on you

- show compassion—care how you feel, especially when you disagree

- support you emotionally

- support you in trying to meet your goals

- try to earn your trust over time

- make compensatory repair

- guarantee your safety

Most of the items on the lists above are self-explanatory. I'll spend the rest of the chapter explaining the ones that are not.

Show Compassion

In my clinical experience, disagreement about "facts" is a major block to the compassion necessary to repair a damaged relationship. Many people have difficulty showing compassion when they disagree with a partner's perspective. This is unfortunate, because compassion is most necessary when there is disagreement. You can often get by with relatively little compassion when you agree, as the agreement itself tends to motivate supportive and reparative behavior. It's when you disagree that sympathy is more necessary to motivate the enormous efforts it takes to repair a relationship damaged by betrayal. When compassion depends on agreement, you are, in effect, saying, "Because I don't agree with your interpretation of the facts, your pain doesn't matter to me," or "You don't have a right to be hurt, because the 'facts' don't support your pain," or worse, "You *should* suffer, because you're wrong."

Of course, most intimate partners who struggle with compassion don't mean any of those things. They are merely confounded by their own guilt or shame, which makes them construe their partners' pain as indictments, rather than cries for understanding and help. As a result, they lapse into defensiveness and abandon the compassion that could help them both.

The key factor in evaluating progress in repair is your partner's ability to show compassion for you, regardless of whether you agree with him.

Support vs. Control

The kind of support that betrayers want to give sometimes seems more like control. In fairness, it's easy to confuse control with support when we feel protective of loved ones. (If you doubt that, just ask your children or a relative for whom you feel a sense of responsibility. What you do out of concern and protectiveness is likely to seem controlling to them.) The lists that follow can help you distinguish support from control in the repair phase of your relationship.

Control implies the following:

- Your perspectives and opinions aren't valid, relevant, or important.

- You are not smart or creative enough to decide things on your own.

- You have to be told what to do and criticized or rejected if you don't do it.

Support respects:

- your perspective and opinions, even when you disagree

- your competence, intelligence, creativity, and resourcefulness

- teamwork in exploring the best course of action

Earn Trust over Time

The betraying partner deserves compassion unconditionally, but trust must be earned. She must show willingness to comply with whatever you, in good faith, from your core value, require to feel safe in the relationship. She should be patient and sensitive to the enormous difficulty of rebuilding trust and not pressure you to renew it before you are ready. (I'll return to this later.)

Make Compensatory Repair

As discussed at length in Chapter 4, emotional healing occurs when the brain associates restorative images with painful memories, so that recurrence of the painful memories automatically invokes the restorative images. Your partner can use this principle to make *compensatory repair*—that is, to supply you with restorative images.

For example, a client I worked with on one of my Oprah Winfrey Show appearances had been quite emotionally abusive to his wife. The most hurtful thing that she could recall him doing—the one that felt the most like utter betrayal—was tearing up several childhood photos of her with various family members. Like most acts of betrayal, this one carried multiple triggers of residual pain. She could be reminded of it whenever she thought of her childhood, her family, or her own children, or when she witnessed other people interacting with their children and families. The possible reminders seemed infinite.

As a gesture of compensatory repair, the man had most of the pictures restored professionally, so that the damage was imperceptible. But he had shredded three or four beyond restoration. For those, he meticulously drew everyone and everything that was in the destroyed pictures. The re-creations took many hours of work over several days. The point of his effort was not artistic verisimilitude; the drawings did not look like the original photos. The image that helped his wife heal was him leaning over a small desk, lit by a single naked lightbulb, determined to draw what was in the pictures, to demonstrate how sorry he was and how important her well-being was to him. She still had reminders of him tearing up the pictures, but now his impulsive tirade was associated with a more measured and meaningful effort to compensate for his atrocious behavior with a sincere expression of love.

In another example, a client's husband discovered her affair just after she had ended it. When he was ready to discuss the possibilities of repair, he told her of the many images he had of her with her lover, whom he'd never seen. He imagined them (obsessed about them) in restaurants, walking hand-in-hand on the sidewalk, drinking together in a bar, embracing, kissing, and making love.

I suggested to my client that she write a letter to her husband, using the following model of compensatory repair. Of course, each client must provide the facts and put the concepts into her own words, provided she can do so honestly and sincerely from her core value.

"Dear _____,

"I am so, so sorry for my egregious violation of my deepest values, which has caused you so much pain. My behavior was unforgivable. I lied to you and broke our vows. Then I had the gall to blame you for my constant irritability, which I now know came from my own guilt and was not related to anything you did. You in no way deserved to be hurt, and I am utterly ashamed of myself for doing these things to you. There is no excuse for my behavior or my failure to consider your feelings. There is no explanation other than my self-destructive moral failings, which I will work hard to correct. I must work my entire life to keep from hurting you in the future. I will not allow my failings to hurt you again."

[Note: the facts of this part of the letter have been changed to protect specific identities.] "You imagined me with Bob in several restaurants, including Bixby's, the one you and I like so much in New York. You imagined me walking with him in Times Square, just as we used to do. You imagined us in a room at the Plaza. You saw me, in your mind, kissing him, embracing him, having sex with him. Honey, I regret so much that you are tormented by those cruel images. I will try my best to replace them with images of you and I being loving and sexual together, images that are filled with the love I have for you. It may be inadequate, but I will try my best to soothe the horribly unfair pain you have suffered. My terrible mistake has made me realize how much I love you and how empty my life would be without you. If you can find it in your heart, please let me try to replace those hurtful images with bright, real-life images of my love for you."

This couple, like most that I have worked with, set about creating restorative images to replace the painful ones embedded in the victim's imagination. The road to recovery was not easy, as his intrusive imaginings occurred on several occasions when they were affectionate with each other. But her compassionate response each time this happened helped them rebuild the life they both deeply wanted.

Compensatory repair is not always possible, of course. I've had a dozen or so cases in which one partner discovered a series of e-mails between a spouse and an interloper. (This has happened often enough to give some credence to the old Freudian notion that some people want to be discovered in their misdeeds.) A few of the discovered e-mails included graphic descriptions of sexual acts, and a few more included explicit photographs of the betrayal. Once a partner reads vivid descriptions of infidelity or sees pictures of it, those incidents are etched in memory, along with the obsessive fantasies that typically grow out of them. It's unlikely that restorative images can be associated with those kinds of toxic imaginings. And yet, only one of those dozen or so marriages broke up because of the affair. In all of the other cases the betrayed partner successfully focused on personal healing and growth, while the betraying partner followed the steps outlined in Part IV of this book. I regard their triumphs as testament to the heroic resilience that enables most of my clients to outgrow devastating personal and relationship wounds.

Guarantee Your Safety

The betrayal you have suffered is evidence that the betrayer lacks sufficient internal inhibitions against violating deeper values. I have worked with thousands of betrayers who have developed those internal inhibitions, through an arduous process of emotion reconditioning. (See the website www.compassionpower.com for more information on emotion reconditioning.) But there is no way that you can be sure that your partner is actually doing the hard work necessary to change emotional habits. In the absence of clear evidence of internal inhibitions, there must be external constraints. Your partner must be willing to promise something drastic that she will suffer, should betrayal recur. Your partner should be willing to say, without hesitation, "If I ever betray you again, I promise to cut off my right arm."

Of course, you would not demand such a drastic consequence if your partner were to stumble again. The point of the declaration is that your partner must show clear determination, without hesitancy, to be true to her deeper values in the future.

The next chapter will describe a compassionate repair process that works for most of my clients.

Summary

Repairing an intimate relationship that has suffered betrayal is a long and tricky endeavor. You should be clear from the outset why you want to repair it. The reasons why you want to repair it can then guide you through the natural self-doubt that recurs throughout the repair process. You should be clear on what you want from your partner and what your partner can and cannot do for you. This is ultimately the difference between support and self-healing: The latter requires self-compassion and core value work. The former requires that your partner ensure your safety, without hesitation, by whatever means necessary.

CHAPTER 14

The Compassionate Repair Process

This chapter offers a comypassionate process for rebuilding betrayed relationships. It includes several formal agreements, which the betraying partner should present to the betrayed. If executed faithfully, these agreements will significantly reduce the probability of future betrayal.

Time Dimensions of Repair

Couples struggling to repair betrayed relationships are sometimes misled by short-term "honeymoons" of reconnection. The great challenge in repair is not *feeling* the attachment emotions of interest, trust, compassion, and love at any point in time; it's *sustaining* them over the long run. Doubt and anxiety inevitably undermine honeymoons and the ability to sustain the attachment emotions. It's best to rebuild slowly, on a solid foundation that can withstand occasional bouts of doubt and anxiety.

It's helpful to think of repair as a process with separate time dimensions, each with characteristic behaviors. Both partners should be clear from the outset about which behaviors belong in the *past* and which are necessary in the *present* to bring about the *future* you both want. Blaming and threats to safety, as well as disrespectful, dishonest, or defensive behavior will certainly bring back the past. You must replace them with behaviors that show responsibility, respect, value, support, honesty, and openness. Only when these are firmly established can you expect to move into a future of sustained intimacy and trust.

Note: Even if the betrayal was a one-time occurrence, such as a one-night stand on a business trip, it's likely that some of the behaviors characterized here as "the past" occurred before the betrayal.

THE PAST	THE PRESENT	THE FUTURE
blame	responsibility	responsibility
danger	safety	safety
disrespect	respect	respect
dishonesty	honesty	honesty
lack of compassion	compassion	compassion
criticism	support	support
stonewalling/ defensiveness	openness	openness
hurt feelings	showing value	showing value
emotional harm	mutual growth	mutual growth
		sustained trust
		sustained intimacy

Notice that sustained intimacy follows sustained trust. Intimacy requires letting down defenses, and it's difficult to do that consistently, without trust.

The ability to sustain trust and intimacy takes a long time to restore after intimate betrayal, even when the present includes all the behaviors listed above. The slowness is due in large part to the recurring cycles that exist in just about all relationships.

Relationship Cycles

The notion of relationship cycles came into public awareness in the 1980s when the "cycle of violence" gained currency in the popular press. The cycle of violence was described as having four discreet stages: tension between the partners builds, climaxing in a violent incident, followed by the remorse and honeymoon phase, in which the couple feels closer for a while, before resuming their normal routine. At that point tension begins to build again, and the cycle continues. After a few iterations of the cycle, the honeymoon stage typically drops out, but the rest of the cycle endures, with the tension stage growing longer in duration, until it seems constant.

Nonabusive relationships have similar, though less dramatic, cycles, due in part to the propensity of the human brain to form habits and patterns of behavior. In our high-stress world, with its many pressures and distractions, partners often form habits of drifting apart, until the occurrence of exceptional distress, such as illness, problems at work, quarrels with friends or neighbors, trouble with the children, death in the family, or conflicts with members of either partner's family of origin. These periods of distress bring the partners closer for a time, before habit-ridden routine resumes control of the relationship.

Typical Relationship Cycle

Routine

Closeness

Stress

Distress

Duration of the Cycle

The length of the repair process is determined in part by the duration of past relationship cycles, particularly the average length of the intervals between each stage within the cycle. Typically, the "distance" and "routine" stages get longer with time, while the others stay more or less the same.

For at least several months into the repair process, the betrayed partner's overstressed central nervous system simply cannot know whether the behavioral improvements of the "present" are not just a manifestation of another interval before the cycle of distance and danger resumes. In fact, a number of cycles have to go by with no repeat of the "past" behaviors before the central nervous system can let down defenses enough to sustain intimacy and trust. In my clinical experience, the average repair time is equal to about three complete cycles, with no behaviors of the "past" recurring. If it took three months for your past cycles to complete (that's the short end of the range in my experience), it will probably take at least nine months for reasonable trust and intimacy to return. If the normal cycle took a year (the higher end of the range), full recovery may take upwards of three years.

It really matters little how much a betrayed partner wants to trust; her brain will not let her drop defenses completely until at least a few cycles of uninterrupted compassion and understanding go by. The betrayer will have to maintain compassion, patience, and understanding, even when—*especially* when—the betrayed partner cannot reciprocate. For quite a while there may be little reward from the betrayed partner, especially if post-traumatic stress symptoms are a factor, as they usually are in betrayed relationships. For repair to be successful, the "distress" stage must be dominated by compassion.

Repair Cycles

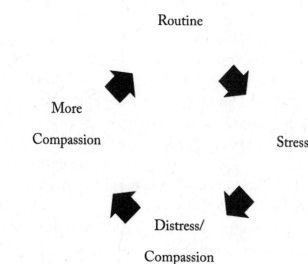

Routine

More
Compassion

Stress

Distress/
Compassion

Compassion vs. Trust

The best way to approach trust in a betrayed relationship is to forget about it until you have time to make decisions based on wise trust. That's right—it's best to put trust on the back burner for a while. Merely attempting to trust while you're still hurt raises fear and anxiety exponentially, undermining all attempts to trust. Lasting trust is not a goal so much as a by-product of enhanced core value. Focus first on self-compassion and then on compassion for each other, and you'll find that trust will sneak up on you, in its own good time, provided your partner behaves honestly and compassionately—in other words, proves trustworthy. You'll wake up one day, many months from now, and realize that you trust your partner again. Before reviewing some of the things that have to happen for trust to "sneak up on you," let me give you an example of compassion without trust.

My late mother was the model for me of how to be wisely compassionate. One Thanksgiving I came home from college to find that she had taken in a couple of distant cousins who were out of work. I was not surprised to see people living in our house. (My mother had overcome severe battering at the hands of my father to become a compassionate person of enormous charity and generosity.) What shocked me was that the closets and drawers in all the rooms, including my bedroom, were locked. I insisted on knowing why. My mother explained, with embarrassment, that my cousins—her distant nephews—had stolen money from her, along with a few pieces of her costume jewelry, and even some of her clothing. Enraged at their ungrateful betrayal, I was ready to throw out the freeloading petty criminals. But she stopped me cold.

"It's not hard to keep things locked," she said. "It would be harder to make them leave when they don't have anywhere to go."

I have used my mother's lesson repeatedly, in my own life and in my work with clients who struggle with intimate betrayal: you can be compassionate without trusting. And the more compassionate you are, the wiser your eventual trust will be. Compassion gives your partner a chance to earn back trust over time with consistently trustworthy behavior.

Wise trust in a betrayed intimate relationship cannot be expected to return fully until self-compassion and core value have grown larger than the fear of being hurt again. At that point your unconscious will have made a judgment about the probability of betrayed trust. In other words, trust will have snuck up on you. Until then, follow the advice of a wise politician: Trust, but verify.

The Compassionate Repair Process

Of course, the most crucial question in regard to repair is this: What will it take for you to feel safe in opening your heart again?

The compassionate repair process should begin with you, the betrayed partner, presenting a list of behaviors that will help you feel safe. Title your list "What I Want You to Do to Help Me Feel Safe in Opening My Heart to You." Don't be passive in compiling your list. Think of what will help you invest emotionally and behaviorally in a vibrant life. (It may be helpful to take a few minutes to run through your core value bank before completing your list.)

After you have completed your list, read it out loud, preferably into a digital recorder. There's nothing like the objectivity and, ultimately, the conviction that a recording can bring.

What the Betrayer Agrees to Do

The following are the agreements that the betrayer should make, both to show good faith in the repair process and to reinforce his motivation to be the best partner he can be.

Compassionate Commitment

Because I care about you and our relationship, I will make a supreme effort to be compassionate to you.

- I will recognize that when I feel resentful or angry, I'm really hurt, anxious, or uncomfortable, and that you are most likely hurt, anxious, or uncomfortable too.

- I will care when you are hurt, anxious, or uncomfortable.

- I will try hard to heal my hurt, regulate my anxiety, and improve my discomfort, and I will support your efforts to do the same.

- I will always tell you the truth and be honest with you in every way.

- I will always treat you with value and respect, even when I disagree with you or do not like your behavior.

- I will always appreciate the unique qualities you bring to our relationship.

- I will not criticize or ignore you.

- I will not try to control, manipulate, coerce, threaten, or intimidate you, or purposely make you feel bad in any way.

- I will try hard to discover and correct the blind spots of my behavior.

- I will try hard to understand your perspective and sympathize with your feelings, especially when I disagree with you.

- I will stay true to my deepest values and try hard to be the best person and partner I can be.

Signature:

The betrayer should read his "Compassionate Commitment" out loud to his partner and give her a signed copy.

We all want to be trusted. There's no question that distrust breeds anxiety, defensiveness, resentment, and anger. Although the natural distrust after betrayal is a burden to the betrayer who wants to rebuild her relationship, it is also an opportunity to show that she can regulate her reflexive responses with compassion. She must sympathize with how difficult it is to trust after betrayal. She should understand that insisting on trust shows a lack of compassion, which, in her partner's mind, raises the probability of future betrayal. A recovering couple can arrive at a place of wise trust much sooner if there is no rush to get there. In other words, the betrayer will get the trust she wants more quickly if she takes the burden of trust off the shoulders of the betrayed. I highly recommend that the betrayer write out the following, sign it, wrap it in special gift wrap, and give it to her partner.

Relief from the Burden of Trust

Please do not trust me until you feel completely comfortable doing so. It is my great hope that we will one day arrive at that point, but I will love and support you no matter how long it takes for us to get there.

Signature: _____

Both the betrayed and the betrayer should read the above out loud to emphasize its importance.

The betrayer responds. In response to the list you created ("What I Want You to Do to Help Me Feel Safe in Opening My Heart to You"), your betrayer should make his own list, titled "What I Will Do to Help You Feel Safe." It should begin with "I hereby agree to try to earn your trust over time by doing, to the best of my ability, what you have said you want me to do to help you feel safe in opening your heart to me." Then he should list all the things you asked of him, and add his signature underneath.

The couple should read the statement and list together aloud, with emphatic declaration—recovery from betrayal cannot be halfhearted.

Statement of compassion. This is an exercise in genuine pride for the betrayer. It shows the difference between what she was in the past and what she has become in the present.

It's a necessary exercise for two reasons. First, it helps associate corrective behavior with mistakes of the past (as part of this book's continuing effort to retrain the brain to make new associations for beneficial behavioral choices). Equally as important, the exercise is an attempt to pull back from a dangerous crossing of "inhibition thresholds."

Although inhibition thresholds have been studied predominantly in areas of physical violence, crime, and compulsive behaviors, there is considerable clinical evidence to suggest that, once we cross such a threshold by doing something we had previously been inhibited to do, we are more likely to continue doing the undesired behavior than to stop. This likelihood is due to the heightened stimulation effect of crossing forbidden barriers. Once a new level of neural stimulation becomes a plateau, more stimulation is necessary for the brain to produce soothing neurotransmitters that cause quiescence or satisfaction. Escalating frequency of behaviors beyond a previous inhibition is a form of "stimulus seeking" (Mawson 1999). You may have noticed that if you go off your diet once, you're more likely to do it again than to stop. People who lie once are more likely to continue lying than to stop. Those who shoplift once are more likely to do it again than to stop. If you're abusive, you're more likely to escalate abuse than to stop (Babcock and Steiner 1999).

I call this neural-stimulation effect, which leads us to violate our deeper values by repeating previously inhibited behaviors, the *bite of the vampire*. Crossing the line of intimate betrayal gives us fangs, which we must continuously keep retracted. Keeping the fangs retracted in the future is the goal of the Statement of Compassion, below.

Statement of Compassion

On a sheet of paper, state how you hurt your partner. List all instances of deceit; financial manipulation; infidelity; and verbal, emotional, or physical abuse. Next to each item, write what you will do differently now and in the future, should similar circumstances occur.

Describe the effects of your behavior on your partner, especially on her capacity to sustain the attachment emotions of interest, compassion, trust, and intimacy.

Describe the effects of your behavior on you, especially on your capacity to sustain the attachment emotions of interest, compassion, trust, and intimacy.

State specifically what you need to do to keep your "fangs" retracted in the future so that you will never intentionally hurt your partner. (This should be a recapitulation of all that you have learned in this book, as well as anything else that can help you be the person and partner you most want to be in the present and future.)

The above should be read aloud by the betrayer to her partner.

Here is what I will do if I ever betray you again. The betrayer should sign, date, and present the following statement to his partner:

I hereby promise that if I ever betray you again, I will cut off my right arm.

Signature: _____

Date: _____

The above agreements will greatly reduce the probability of betrayed trust. But keep this in mind: to heal, improve, and repair, we can't just "talk the talk"; we have to "walk the walk." Repair does not happen through occasional words; it occurs only with consistent behavior.

The Secret of Recovery

The following is a fictionalized composite of several different client stories, designed to illustrate crucial points about rebuilding a betrayed relationship.

On the second day of his honeymoon, James woke up in the middle of the night and was startled when he saw the empty place beside him where his bride had been sleeping. Tisa didn't answer his calls, and he couldn't find her anywhere in their beach bungalow. By the time he ran outside to look for her, he was panicked. He walked in one direction and saw nothing, then turned and started running the opposite way. He noticed a lantern. As he ran toward it, he saw in the moonlight that Tisa, in her nightgown, was talking to the man holding the lantern. His fear instantly turned to fury. He sprinted toward them as fast as he could and, as soon as he was within earshot, accused his wife of having planned a midnight rendezvous with the stranger. The "man" in the moonlight turned out to be a twelve-year-old boy. Fearing for his safety, the boy dropped the lantern and ran away.

"He's just a child," Tisa pleaded.

"That makes it worse! It's practically our wedding day, you slut!"

Tisa felt for a fleeting moment that she might not leave the beach alive—her husband's anger was that intense.

She tried her best that night, and many times for many years thereafter, to explain the encounter to James. She couldn't sleep because she was so excited and happy about their new life together. She went for a walk on the beautiful beach, where she met the native boy, who was gathering nocturnal crabs. He was explaining to her how to lure them into the lantern light with tiny pieces of fish, when they heard James shouting.

Most of the time, James was rational enough to accept this obvious explanation. But for reasons he couldn't entirely understand, he never trusted Tisa after that night. For the next eleven years, she walked on eggshells, never sure when his jealousy would flare up again. She had to account for almost every minute of her time and had to take care not to be courteous—much less friendly—to waiters and service men in his presence.

"I felt like a suspect in a crime, or a fugitive from the 'don't smile at men' police," she told me.

James was just as tormented by his Jekyll and Hyde vacillations between logical reality and totally irrational jealousy. It was only when Tisa finally realized that his treatment of her was a betrayal of his promise to love, honor, and cherish that she prepared to leave him. He subsequently attended one of my Love without Hurt Boot Camps for chronic resentment, anger, and emotional abuse. After considerable core value work, he made all the agreements outlined in this chapter.

How They Rebuilt Trust

Several months after he completed the boot camp, James and Tisa were dressing to go to a party. James could see that Tisa was nervous. This was the first party they were to attend since his treatment. Before the boot camp, he had thought that the tension he felt whenever they prepared to go somewhere was in reaction to *her* tension; she was always late, always distracted or worried about something, he thought. Now he understood that on those previous, unhappy occasions, they were both worried about what would happen if she talked for more than a couple of minutes to a man at the party.

On this night, he brought her a flower from the garden as she was getting ready for the party and tried to reassure her that everything would be fine. He was convinced there would be no problem—if he felt any of the old jealousy, he would use the skills he learned in the boot camp. Because those skills are harder to access under the influence of alcohol, he promised not to touch a drop.

James stayed true to his word about drinking. Yet, to his deep disappointment, the old jealous feelings came back when he saw his attractive wife casually talking to different men at the party. He said nothing about it to Tisa. He didn't have to.

On the drive home, neither said a word for the first few miles. Tisa was once again second-guessing herself—not as bad as when she had been walking on eggshells before James attended the boot camp— but nevertheless, she told herself that she shouldn't have talked to *any* man at the party, let alone one as handsome as Tim. She blamed herself for the resentment she saw in James's face and worried that he would soon relapse. She was right about James's resentment, but it wasn't directed at her. He was angry at himself for allowing his jealousy to flare up again. He, too, was thinking how he *should* have responded.

James tried to explain to me the next day that the wind blew the front door closed behind them as they walked in the house, and that's why it made such a loud noise. Anger at himself was the likely explanation of how the door got slammed, but that's not the one that occurred to Tisa. The door slamming startled her, and the adrenaline rush that followed turned her anxiety to anger.

"I am so sick of this crap!" she screamed. "Why did I ever think you would change? How *stupid* could I be?"

James pretended not to know what she meant—a remnant of their walking-on-eggshells days. "*What* are you talking about?"

"I am so sick of you!" she screamed. "All you ever think about is yourself. You're supposed to be compassionate now? Compassion my ass! You haven't changed one single bit."

"You know how hard I've worked," he protested.

"I know how hard you *say* you've worked, but you're just as much of a Neanderthal as ever. I was just so stupid to think you could be different."

"You don't think I've changed at all?" He was astonished and defensive—a serious lapse of self-compassion, which led to a failure of compassion for Tisa.

"This whole 'compassion' thing is just another one of your *manipulations*," she shouted. "Who wouldn't want to be with another man, after living with you? A real man would never put his wife through what I've been through with you!"

James had never seen this much rage and disgust from his petite, usually demure wife. He turned away from her and tried to imagine the contents of his core value bank.

"Go ahead, turn away," she shouted. "Act like a goddamn wimp!"

She continued to shout for a while, while James tried hard to do his core value work.

"It was all those years of hell pouring out of me," Tisa told me on the phone the next day. "I knew I was taunting him but couldn't stop myself."

"What did James do?" I asked. (She had started the phone call by saying they "had a *near* blowup last night." I worried about what she meant by "near.")

"He gave me a while," she said. "A few minutes, an hour, I don't know. Then he came and sat down next to me. I told him I didn't want him touching me just then, and he didn't."

"What did he do?" I asked again.

"I'll never forget it," she said with a sudden lump in her throat.

Even though he sensed that she couldn't stand to look at him, he found the courage to tell her, "I know that I've hurt you so much in the past and that it will take a long, long time for you to trust me again. I want you to know that I will do all I can to help you heal and won't expect you to trust me at all, until you feel ready. And if you never do, I will still love you and be there for you the best I can."

"You were feeling it again—that crap again," she said, but in a much less accusatory tone.

"I did feel some of the old jealousy," he admitted. "But that's my problem to deal with, not yours. Don't you even think about trying to protect me from it—I have to learn to handle it. I can't promise that I won't feel it again, but I do promise that I'll never take it out on you again."

I got a lump in my throat when Tisa told me this. Still, I had to warn her, "This kind of thing is going to come up again—those feelings are so automatic and so entrenched in both your heads. But if he can show compassion for you each time, you'll have an excellent chance of rebuilding your relationship."

She didn't really want to hear just then that it would still take a long time to recover. "Will I *ever* trust him again?" she asked with discernible sadness in her voice.

"Eventually you'll form new habits in response to his respectful and compassionate behavior. But it will take a long time of him meeting each one of your hurt and angry reactions with compassion and reparative behavior." She said nothing, but I could tell that her sadness remained. "Keep focused on the future," I told her. "But always remember, whether or not he comes through with compassion each time, you still must feel compassion for yourself to heal those old hurts. And eventually you will."

Although this was a composite account, the psychological issues of the story are common in rebuilding betrayed relationships. It would have been disastrous had James blamed Tisa for her reactions. What if he'd told her, "You're making too much of it," or "Stop living in the past," or "Get over it, already," or if he'd gotten defensive or aggressive in any way? Had he yielded to those defensive impulses, he would have proven to Tisa that she couldn't trust him to be compassionate and, therefore, couldn't safely love him. Just as important, he would not have been able to trust himself to maintain compassion for her during the long, complicated healing process, in which she would be revisited many times by powerful memories of past hurt, just as he would be revisited by his recurring feelings of jealousy. He was able to show support for her PTS symptoms and thereby show her that the probability of betrayed trust in the future had faded.

Significantly, the clients whose details were meshed together in the above account, like almost all those I have worked with, found that their decision to focus on compassion instead of trust worked for them. It took an average of two years to realize that, just by responding to the routine changes in their partners' "present" behaviors over time, they had started trusting again, without trying.

Summary

In attempting to repair a betrayed relationship, it's helpful to distinguish among behaviors that belong in the past (blame, dishonesty, disrespect), the present (compassion, responsibility, safety, respect, honesty) and a future of increased intimacy and trust. The natural relationship cycles of routine, distance, and closeness drag out the repair process, as a distressed central nervous system cannot tell if present behavioral improvements are merely products of an interval before the danger stage of the cycle. Roughly three of your typical cycles have to go by without any of the behaviors of the "past" for intimacy and trust to return. Compassion is the key. The "Compassionate Repair Process" consists of a series of solemn agreements the betrayer makes to the betrayed partner.

CHAPTER 15

The Reconnection Dilemma

Deciding that you want to rebuild your relationship with the partner who betrayed you settles only half your dilemma. You still have to determine the level of emotional reconnection you want to pursue. This chapter will help you begin to establish reconnection on whichever level you choose, whether it be deeper or shallower than the connection you had before the betrayal.

The British psychiatrist John Bowlby (1969, 1973, 1977, 1980) gave us *attachment theory* as a way of understanding how emotional bonds are formed early in life and, to a lesser extent, how they are maintained in adulthood. The word *attachment* aptly describes the effects of intimate relationships on our minds and bodies. It feels like our lovers are literally attached to us, like we've "got them under our skin." When betrayal tears a couple apart, it's as if a portion of their flesh is ripped away.

In my clinical experience, the long and difficult healing process forms a kind of psychological scar tissue over the traumatized area of previous connection, preventing reconnection on that same level. Metaphors aside, your relationship will quite literally never be the same. If you choose to rebuild, your options are to attempt reconnection either on a more superficial level or on a deeper plane than you had before the betrayal.

Most couples recovering from betrayal choose to reconnect more superficially, with less affection, interest, and trust. This can be a viable choice when there are children for whom relationship dissolution could be traumatic. It can also serve both parties well if companionship or close friendship is a mutual goal. For some couples, the choice to reconnect more superficially is temporary, to give them time to decide whether they want to deepen their connection or go their separate ways.

Couples who are able to form a deeper connection after betrayal report that the trauma, along with the likelihood of losing the relationship, made them realize how important they were to each other. The great threat of loss made their union more precious to them and worthy of the hard work of repair.

Attitude of Connection

You will more likely achieve the level of reconnection you decide is right for you by adopting an *attitude of connection*.

Part belief and part emotion, *attitudes* are evaluations based on personal values or preferences. If your goal is to repair a damaged relationship, it's advisable to base your attitudes on how much you value a connection with your partner over the long run, rather than how you feel about her at the moment. Your feelings will probably continue to be confusing, with at least a subtle undercurrent of doubt and anxiety about the decision to reconnect. The values component of attitudes organizes feelings into a more coherent whole that is more easily regulated by the prefrontal cortex, the brain's hub for rational analysis, judgment, willpower, and the ability to make decisions in your long-term best interests.

Elements of Connection Attitudes

Attitudes of connection have the following key elements:

- Focus on the relationship you want.

- Regard yourself as connected.

- Behave as if you're connected.

- Use binocular vision.

- Practice tolerance.

- Root your connection in common values.

- Build lifelines.

- Establish routine rituals of connection.

Focus on the Relationship You Want

Recovery will bog down if you become preoccupied with thoughts of how the relationship has deteriorated or with speculation about possible causes of the betrayal. It's much more productive to focus on what you want your relationship to be in the future than what it was in the past. Of course, this advice is easier said than done—the human brain tends to replay past hurts as long as there is fear of similar hurt in the future. Don't blame yourself for these thoughts, but try not to indulge them. Be patient with yourself in the process and keep focused on your deepest values. For a guide, use the exercise in Chapter 13 titled "What I Want from My Partner" and the one in Chapter 12 titled "The Partner I Want to Become."

Regard Yourself as Connected

Connection is essentially a mental state and a choice. You choose to be connected and you choose to be disconnected. Constructive change in behavior is more likely when it's encouraged by an attitude of connection, rather than discouraged by attitudes of disconnection, which are usually fueled by anger, disgust, or shame. Below is a way to express the key differences in attitudes about connection.

Attitude of disconnection: "I can't connect with you unless you do what I want."

Attitude of connection: "I want to maintain our connection, but we have to... (example: respect each other) to protect the connection we both value."

With an attitude of connection, you think in terms of "us" and "ours," rather than "me," "you," "mine," and "yours." Not surprisingly, research shows that partners in happy relationships tend to use the "couple" pronouns, while those in unhappy unions opt for the "single" pronouns (Seider et al. 2009). At first it may seem awkward to make this semantic shift when you feel negatively about your partner. But working "us" and "ours" into your everyday vocabulary will help you reach your goal by reinforcing an attitude of connection. Try writing this sentence three times to see how it feels to you:

> "*We* have work to do on *our* relationship, so it can bring *us* the safety and security *we* both want and deserve."

If the couple mode of thinking becomes more comfortable, you're moving closer to repair.

Behave as if You Were Connected

A tried and true behavioral therapy technique is *behaving as if* the change you want has already occurred. Think of how many times you've heard someone say, for instance, "When I feel better, I'll start to exercise." Almost always, people feel better *after* they start to exercise and not before. Behavior change tends to change feelings more often than the other way around. This is not always true, of course, but I have seen it succeed far more often than it has failed. When you behave as if you were connected, you're likely to think in terms of couplehood and, eventually, feel more connected. I urge you to try it just as an experiment for the next month. Practice every day what you write in the following exercise:

List what you would do if you felt more connected to your partner (for example: touch more, make more eye contact, embrace more, go for walks together).

Also practice, every day for the next month, what you write in this exercise:

THE HAPPY MARRIAGE PILL

The Happy Marriage Pill can be taken in the form of an ordinary low-dose aspirin (which is also good for your heart). Take the Happy Marriage Pill tonight, and you'll wake up tomorrow happily married and totally satisfied with your relationship.

On a piece of paper, describe three things you would do differently if you woke up tomorrow happily married and totally satisfied with your relationship.

Do whatever you wrote above, *every day*, and you should feel at least a little more connected after a month. You cannot wait for your relationship to become happy before you change your behavior. Relationships improve after behavior changes, not before.

Use Binocular Vision

Binocular vision is the ability to see your partner's perspective alongside your own and to see yourself through your partner's eyes. In other words, you see your relationship through two perspectives at once.

To appreciate the importance of seeing your partner's point of view, while maintaining your own, compare *monocular* with *binocular* vision. Looking through one eye (monocular vision) cuts your cone of vision in half. More important, it distorts depth perception and impairs the ability to judge speed and direction of movement. It's hard to realize this just by covering up one eye, because your brain fills in the missing information with estimates of what the other eye would see. It's easier to grasp the difference by comparing binoculars—which give a wide visual spectrum—with telescopes, which magnify within the radius of a small circle. With binoculars you get a fairly accurate sense of how far away an object is, relative to other objects in the spectrum. You can better judge the speed and direction of movement, because objects move across the plane of the spectrum. A telescope, on the other hand, magnifies all objects within the circle equally. You have to keep moving the glass as the magnified object moves, and doing so impairs the sense of dynamism—speed and direction of movement. Thus the development of binoculars was a boon to military strategists, though somewhat less fortunate for opposing troops who became easier targets of artillery barrages.

Perceptions of depth and dynamism in relationships, as in optics, are unique products of binocular vision. Only binocular vision can give an accurate picture of your relationship, allowing you to see more deeply into the heart of your partner, while observing your part in the interactive cycle. In any given interaction, we all have blind spots concerning our emotionally charged perceptions and behavior. Our own actions, which are mostly reflexive and habituated, do not get encoded in memory with anything like the intensity or vividness of the behavior of loved ones. On automatic pilot, we simply cannot see what they are reacting to, and so their reactions may seem irrational. Binocular vision allows the partners to see themselves through each other's eyes.

It's absolutely imperative to identify your blind spots, own them without being defensive, and adjust your behavior to compensate for them. For instance, a notorious blind spot of mine is thinking about what I have to do next while my partner is talking about her day. I used to be defensive when she accused me of not listening, because I was sure that I was; after all, I could repeat everything she said. Of course, hearing is not the same as listening. I have learned to acknowledge that mind wandering is something I do completely without awareness—in other words, it's my blind spot. I appreciate it when she points it out to me, because I do not want her to feel unheard.

My clients often resist binocular vision at first, out of fear that they will lose something if they truly understand their partners' perspectives. They sometimes confuse binocular vision with simple perspective taking, which is a largely ineffective relationship tool (Gottman 1995). As Vorauer and Sucharyna (2012) explain it, perspective takers overestimate their own transparency in regard to their values, preferences, traits, and feelings. They lose self-evaluation acuity—develop more blind spots—and create more discrepancies between their partners' and their own experience of their exchanges. These discrepancies prompt more negative responses, leaving both dissatisfied. With binocular vision, you never give up your perspective; you *add* to it, through a deeper understanding of your partner's. Like self-compassion and compassion for loved ones, the two perspectives of a close relationship must be kept in balance.

Think of binocular vision as a way to add new dimensions to your experience. It makes you smarter. In the wild, the more intelligent animals have binocular vision—eyes in the front of their heads—which better equips them for seeing movement and judging distances. Prey animals, like deer and antelope, have one eye on either side of their heads, and thereby suffer a distinct disadvantage in vision, which they make up for with the size of their herds—what they lack in acuity they make up for in quantity. Part of the reason that prey animals are more nervous and skittish, even when they're in captivity and have never seen a predator, is that they cannot trust their vision to give them enough information to know when they are safe. Monocular vision increases anxiety. In human relationships, monocular perspectives breed nervousness and suspicion. When you lapse into monocular vision, you can feel that your partner is out to make your life miserable.

Never trust your own perspective if you cannot see your partner's alongside it. Even if completely correct, your perspective is incomplete, lacking depth and dynamism. The only complete reality of your relationship is both perspectives together.

Due to the powerful reactivity of negative emotions, you have an automatic internal sensor of your partner's emotional experience. Here's a general guide, which should always be verified with your partner:

- I'm frustrated, which means my partner probably feels frustrated too.

- I feel rejected, which means my partner probably feels overwhelmed or distracted.

- I feel controlled, which means my partner probably feels anxious or out of control.

A good way to develop (or reawaken) your ability to perceive your partner's internal world is to fill out the answers below.

Binocular Vision Regulation

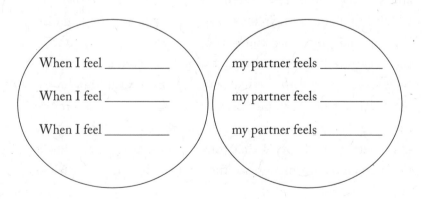

When I feel _____   my partner feels _____

When I feel _____   my partner feels _____

When I feel _____   my partner feels _____

Don't forget to check out your binocular vision answers with your partner, to ensure that you're accurate in describing his feelings: "Did I get this right? When I feel *this* way is it likely you are feeling *that* way?"

Sometimes it's difficult for one or both partners in recovering couples to see the other's perspective sufficiently to begin practicing binocular vision. This is particularly true in cases where chronic resentment has desensitized the parties to the internal worlds of each other, replacing the natural sensitivity of compassion with demonization—assuming the worst about the other. ("He's narcissistic," "She's borderline," "He's domineering," "She's abusive.") So instead of binocular vision (I feel bad; my partner must feel bad too), you assume that your partner feels great or benefits in some way because you feel bad.

If this is the case for you, sometimes a simple trick, like becoming the defense lawyer for your partner (instead of the prosecutor), can help.

ADVOCACY EXERCISE

In this exercise, each partner becomes the lawyer for the other, passionately presenting the other partner's case (perspective).

On a piece of paper, write the statement "Ladies and gentlemen of the jury, my client (partner) suffered in the following ways from intimate betrayal:" Then list all the ways you can think of that your partner has suffered.

The advocacy exercise should help you see the effects of the betrayal on your partner—irrespective of who was the betrayed and who was the betrayer. If you have a hard time with the exercise, run through the boxes of your CVB and try it again.

Practice Tolerance

Tolerance in intimate relationships is the ability to accept your partner's opinions, emotional states, and behaviors when they differ from yours. The high emotional reactivity that typically follows intimate betrayal tends to make partners particularly intolerant of any kind of negative emotions in each other. As a result, neither has room to self-regulate; a negative feeling in one causes chaos or shutdown in the other. The inability to tolerate emotional states that differ from your own will surely impede progress toward repair.

Tolerance of differences is integral to negotiation about specific behaviors. Without tolerance, negotiation can easily deteriorate into pleading, demanding, or coercing.

The Tolerance Scale below, filled out weekly for the next several weeks, will help you internalize the importance of tolerance in maintaining a positive emotional connection.

EXERCISE: Tolerance Scale

On a piece of paper, copy the list below, and for each item indicate the current level of tolerance in your relationship, as well as the level you would like to reach in the future, using this scale: 2 = tolerance; 1 = mild tolerance; 0 = no tolerance.

My partner's tolerance of me when:

_____ I am hyper and she is calm, or vice versa

_____ I am serious and she is joking, or vice versa

_____ I am neat and she is messy, or vice versa

_____ I want to plan and she wants to be spontaneous, or vice versa

_____ I am punctual and she is laid back, or vice versa

_____ I am worried and she is distracted, or vice versa

_____ I want to hug and she wants space, or vice versa

_____ I want to express emotions and she wants to chill out, or vice versa

_____ I am talky and she is quiet, or vice versa

_____ I am romantic and she is not, or vice versa

_____ I am interested in something and she is bored, or vice versa

_____ I have a strong opinion or preference that she disagrees with, or vice versa

My tolerance of my partner when:

_____ She is hyper and I am calm, or vice versa

_____ She is serious and I am joking, or vice versa

_____ She is neat and I am messy, or vice versa

_____ She wants to plan and I want to be spontaneous, or vice versa

_____ She is punctual and I am laid back, or vice versa

_____ She is worried and I am distracted, or vice versa

_____ She wants to hug and I want space, or vice versa

_____ She wants to express emotions and I want to chill out, or vice versa

_____ She is talky and I am quiet, or vice versa

_____ She is romantic and I am not, or vice versa

_____ *She is interested in something and I am bored, or vice versa*

_____ *She has a strong opinion or preference that I disagree with, or vice versa*

Try to fill out the Tolerance Scale once a week for the next six weeks. Repetition will highlight the importance of tolerance in close relationships. Of course, the key to raising tolerance is for both of you to reinforce your core value. This makes you more self-accepting and less threatened by differences, which, in turn, makes you more accepting of each other.

Root Your Connection in Common Values

Deep connection is not based on shared preferences of what you like and enjoy. Rather, it's based on shared values. Common interests often attract people, but common values sustain relationships. A couple whose connection is based on common interests without common values will likely become competitive in their interests. (Instead of hiking together because they value each other's company and well-being, they will want to see who can hike longer or faster.) Couples almost always share many of the items in their CVBs. That's a great place to look for ways to deepen a connection based on values.

As an exercise in "values connection," make a list of areas of deep connection (based on values) that you might possibly develop in the future. (Try to think in terms of mutual activities, such as joining community groups, sharing spiritual experiences, or traveling.)

As with all the exercises in this book, what you write will need to be put into action to have an optimal effect.

Build Lifelines

Like the lines that astronauts use to keep attached to their space vehicles, emotional lifelines provide maximum movement, while providing lifesaving connection. As a relationship metaphor, lifelines keep us anchored to what matters most.

Imagine a long, flexible lifeline connecting you and your partner. No matter what you're doing or feeling, you remain connected. Even when you're angry at each other, or when you need a time-out to get away from each other, you're still connected. If you imagine a constant connection by an invisible lifeline, your unconscious emotional demeanor around your partner will change for the better, increasing the likelihood of positive response from your partner. Bad moments will occur less frequently and will be shorter-lived, because they won't trigger disconnection.

Make a list of the major ways you are deeply connected to your partner. Title it "My Lifeline to You," and give it to your partner.

Establish Routine Rituals of Connection

Recovery from intimate betrayal depends on routine connection. Small gestures of connection built into your daily routine do wonders to create a stable attitude of connection. In contrast, special events, like romantic weekends or nice vacations, while they may be pleasant or enjoyable, are often followed by a letdown when the unsustainable wave of well-being crashes back to the routine of daily living. Don't get me wrong, romantic weekends, nice vacations, and the like are good for relationships, *if* there is also routine connection. The safety and security that will help you repair your relationship rises from a steady attitude of connection, rather than big waves of emotional experience. The secret to loving big is thinking small.

I have found that change in my clients' behavior becomes permanent when connective behaviors are small enough to fit into a daily routine. To that end, I designed the Power Love Formula, which takes less than five minutes a day. Each iteration should begin with a conscious awareness of why you are doing it—to strengthen your connection. (For the next year or so, the betrayer should initiate the Power Love Formula, with the betrayed partner striving to be receptive but initiating less frequently. When healing is complete, initiation can equalize.)

Step one: make importance gestures. Make some gesture of your partner's importance to you at four crucial times of the day. (As a general rule, behaviors we do during transitional times have more carryover effect, as you are more likely to take your current attitudes into the next circumstance you encounter.)

Your *importance gesture* is a way of keeping your partner close to your heart. Come up with a brief, nonverbal gesture that acknowledges your partner's significance to you. It can be a touch, gentle eye contact, or simply reaching out your hand. (Only the two of you need know what the gesture means. It can be your precious secret.) Make your importance gesture at the four major transitional times of the day:

- as soon as you wake up

- before you leave home

- as soon as you come back home

- just before you go to sleep

One of the best behaviors you can do for your overall health and well-being is affirm your partner's importance to you first thing in the morning. Your second daily acknowledgement—before you leave the house in the morning—creates a positive image of your partner to carry with you while you're apart. The third sets a positive tone for spending the prebedtime hours together. Your final daily acknowledgment will sweeten your dreams and carry your love into the next morning.

Step two: hug six times a day. Hugs are usually the first thing to go when a chain of resentment dominates a relationship. Over time, failure to embrace becomes a prescription for disaster; the less you touch, the more resentful you get, and the more resentful you get, the less you touch. The following routine, which takes thirty-six seconds per day, is designed to reverse this downward momentum.

Hug your partner in a full-body embrace—with as many of your body parts touching as possible—a minimum of six times a day, holding each hug for a minimum of six seconds. (Full-body embrace is one of the few reliable ways that men get oxytocin—the bonding hormone that makes us feel close, connected, calm, and trusting.) The formula is not arbitrary. You probably do not hug more than once or twice a day now. Increasing that to six times per day will facilitate a new level of closeness. The six-second minimum for each hug recognizes the fact that in the beginning, many of those hugs will be forced. Even if they start out forced, they are likely to become genuine at about the fourth or fifth second, provided you're still attached to each other. This kind of embrace also increases levels of serotonin, which helps reduce appetite. Not a bad deal—you'll feel better, with less edginess, irritability, and sadness, and just maybe you'll drop a pound or two in the process of feeling closer.

Step three: indulge positive thoughts about your relationship. This is easy. At some point during your workday, stop for ten seconds to think positive thoughts about your partner. List a few on a piece of paper.

Step four: make a contract. Write the following out as a formal contract. Keep it brief and simple. Carry out the action at an agreed upon time every day. It is a symbolic expression of your love.

I hereby agree to show my love for you every day by (doing one of the following):

1. Lighting a candle for you

2. Posting an "I love you" note

3. Putting a flower petal on your breakfast plate

4. Sending an "I love you" text message

5. Writing one line of our favorite song

6. Other: _____

The simple, daily behaviors of the Power Love Formula will help revitalize your emotional connection. (It is a major predictor of success in one-year follow-ups to our boot camps for betrayed relationships.) But the good it will do is not in any one or several implementations. The overall benefit of the Power of Love Formula lies in the accumulative effect of a steady connection over time.

Caveat: Once you start the Power of Love Formula, you must continue it for at least a year. It will have an overall negative effect if you stop it because you're mad at your partner or because you get bored with it. View it as a relationship commitment. Over time, you'll reap the reward of a closer, more emotionally connected relationship.

Summary

You can choose to reconnect emotionally to the partner who betrayed you, either on a deeper or more superficial level than you were connected before the betrayal. Whichever level you choose will be more easily achieved with an attitude of connection, wherein you regard yourself as connected, focus on how you want your relationship to be in the future, behave as if you are connected, use binocular vision—the ability to see your perspective and your partner's simultaneously—strive to be tolerant, build lifelines, and establish small, routine gestures of connection.

EPILOGUE

Healing, Repair, Forgiveness

There have been many books written about forgiveness, emphasizing various aspects of a very complex concept. My purpose in this brief epilogue is not to add to the voluminous literature on forgiveness but to offer some practical advice about it.

Some authors, writing mostly from religious perspectives, state that you cannot heal without forgiving. After working with thousands of clients, I'm fairly sure that most forgiveness occurs as a by-product of healing rather than a cause of it. You heal and then forgive, not the other way around. Attempting to forgive while in pain is like trying to put out a fire in an oil field without sealing the wells. As long as the pain is present, any forgiveness you achieve will be a temporary elevation of feelings, likely to sink into a pool of defensive resentment or contempt as soon as the unhealed wound flares up again.

Facts about Forgiveness

You can forgive someone who has betrayed you without resuming a relationship. And if you decide to resume it, forgiveness—as an intentional act—is unnecessary to repair it. I have seen a great many successfully repaired relationships with no one saying, "I forgive you."

Forgiveness does not mean condoning or excusing bad behavior. It does not relieve the offender of responsibility or accountability for the offense. If you want to repair the relationship, forgiveness does not relieve your partner of having to earn back your trust through consistent reparative and trustworthy behavior.

Forgiveness requires regulating the impulse to punish, resent, or carry a grudge. In recognition of the harm inflicted on the self by acting on the impulse to punish, resent, or bear grudges, forgiveness becomes an issue of personal health and well-being. Your decision to forgive should be based on what is best for your health and well-being.

If you want to repair, you're not likely to forgive before the repair process is well under way. Your unconscious brain will not commit to permanent forgiveness as long as there is a probability of hurt, as there always is before damaged relationships are at least partially repaired.

The order of emotional milestones is likely to go like this: personal healing, at least partial repair, then forgiveness.

The decision to intentionally forgive, of course, is highly personal. The following discussion of the functions of forgiveness is intended to help you arrive at a decision that is right for you.

Functions of Forgiveness

Forgiveness has two primary functions: religious or spiritual, and relationship detachment.

There are ancient religious and spiritual components to forgiveness as a "soul cleansing" process. It is beyond the purview of a psychology book to go into that element of forgiveness, except to say this: if your personal religious or spiritual beliefs demand forgiveness, it will be to your psychological advantage to consider it carefully, since any violation of a deep personal value brings guilt, shame, and anxiety.

Don't get me wrong—I believe in the psychological reality of "soul cleansing." But it's the betrayer who needs to cleanse his soul, through consistent reparative and compassionate behavior. The betrayed needs to heal, grow, learn, and develop more viable defenses, but she doesn't need to "cleanse the soul" for having been betrayed.

The other primary function of forgiveness is relationship detachment. In the psychological sense most relevant to intimate relationships, detachment from an emotional bond occurs at the point where you become able think about your former lover without significant positive or negative emotion. In other words, you're "over it." That kind of forgiveness is described as bringing "peace." Unfortunately, detachment through forgiveness is rare.

Intimate relationships typically break up with at least one of the partners feeling dumped or wronged, if not betrayed. Detachment under those circumstances comes at the end of a very long period of resentment. Over time, resentment turns into contempt, and contempt eventually turns into the final predetachment emotion of disgust. The literal meaning of *disgust* is to throw up an ingested substance the body perceives as harmful. And that is a good metaphor for attachment that goes bad. We get the former beloved "out of us," like milk gone sour, through disgust.

You may recall this common detachment process in an earlier relationship, particularly a youthful one, for which you've gained objectivity through the passage of time. If you were dumped when you were young, you probably went through a period of intense grief, followed by resentment ("How dare he do this to me!" or "She was outrageously unfair!"), followed by contempt ("She has a personality disorder," or "He's a sociopath," or "Something is seriously wrong with her!"), and, finally, disgust, when you couldn't stand to imagine ever having been intimate with that person. Once the disgust stage passed, you could think of your former lover with little emotion, positive or negative. This process is always long and not usually simple, as so many people get stuck in the resentment or contempt stages without ever detaching. Forgiveness is a more elusive but far more positive way to achieve detachment.

The secret of forgiveness, regardless of whether you want to use it as a method of detachment or as a way to fortify your relationship after repair, is to focus not on the offensive behavior, but on freeing yourself of the emotional pain you experienced as a result of the behavior.

The most severe aspect of emotional pain is the sense of powerlessness it engenders. Intentional forgiveness helps you take back power over your emotional life.

The format of intentional forgiveness I use with my clients who want to achieve it is similar to the strategy for overcoming resentment, as described in Chapter 9. At the end of your healing process, the subtext of forgiveness will be something like this: "I forgive you for reminding me that I sometimes feel devalued, inadequate, and unlovable. I know that I am valuable and worthy of love, because I value and love others. Whenever I think of how you hurt me, I will value someone or something and show love to a significant person in my life, and that will remind me of how valuable and lovable I truly am."

Reclaiming power in this way makes forgiveness relatively easy, once you are completely healed, through core value work. As long as you feel powerless, forgiveness is all but impossible.

In my clinical experience, most lasting forgiveness is passive, not intentional. When you focus on self-compassion and develop your core value, forgiveness, like trust, sneaks up on you, whether in the form of detachment or—if you decide to repair your relationship—in full emotional reinvestment. You'll realize that you have healed your emotional injuries and are able to create the life of value and meaning that you have longed for and that you deserve.

Final Point

Helping you take control of your emotional well-being by controlling the meaning of your experience has been the purpose of this book. Hopefully that strategy has brought you to the point where you have grown larger than your hurt, or at least to where you can see progress toward that end. Much of the book is based on recent neurological findings: how the brain forms habits and grows new cells through focus and repetition, and how we can wisely guide our neurological development by choosing what to focus on and what to repeat, in accordance with our deepest values. But the initial inspiration of the book predated the revolution in brain science.

A wonderfully insightful woman in the early history of family therapy, through sheer genius and without the benefit of advancements in neurology and brain imaging, seemed to know all that we have since learned. Virginia Satir (1983) compared life to a garden with rocks and flowers. We can't do much about the rocks of life—whether people lie to us, cheat on us, steal from us, hurt us, or otherwise betray us. If we focus on the rocks, life will be bleak and forlorn. But we can always plant more flowers (create more value). The more flowers we grow, the less important the rocks are, and the more enriched life becomes. The human psyche heals itself by planting more flowers.

References

Babcock, J. C., and R. Steiner. 1999. "The Relationship between Treatment, Incarceration, and Recidivism of Battering: A Program Evaluation of Seattle's Coordinated Community Response to Domestic Violence." *Journal of Family Psychology* 13: 46–59.

Baron, R. A. 1984. "The Control of Human Aggression: An Optimistic Overview." *Journal of Social and Clinical Psychology* 69: 97–119.

Baron, R. A. 1984. "Reducing Organizational Conflict: An Incompatible Response Approach." *Journal of Applied Psychology* 69: 272–79.

Bowlby, J. 1969. *Attachment*. Vol. 1 of *Attachment and Loss*. New York: Basic Books.

Bowlby, J. 1973. *Separation: Anxiety and Anger*. Vol. 2 of *Attachment and Loss*. New York: Basic Books.

Bowlby, J. 1977. "The Making and Breaking of Affectional Bonds: I. Etiology and Psychopathology in the Light of Attachment Theory." *British Journal of Psychiatry* 130: 201–10.

Bowlby, J. 1980. *Loss: Sadness and Depression*. Vol. 3 of *Attachment and Loss*. New York: Basic Books.

Brickman, P., D. Coates, and R. Janoff-Bulman. 1978. "Lottery Winners and Accident Victims: Is Happiness Relative?" *Journal of Personality and Social Psychology* 36: 917–27.

Byrne, G. J., B. Raphael, and E. Arnold. 1999. "Alcohol Consumption and Psychological Distress in Recently Widowed Older Men." *Australian and New Zealand Journal of Psychiatry* 33: 740–47.

Coontz, S. 2006. *Marriage, a History: How Love Conquered Marriage.* New York: Penguin Books.

Diener, E. 2009. "Subjective Well-Being." *Social Indicators Research Series* 37: 11–58.

Eldridge, K. A. and A. Christensen. 2002. "Demand-Withdraw Communication during Couple Conflict: A Review and Analysis." In *Understanding Marriage: Developments in the Study of Couple Interaction,* edited by P. Noller and J. A. Feeney, 289–322. New York: Cambridge University Press.

Gottman, J., C. Rabin, R. Levenson, L. Carstensen, N. Jacobson, and R. Rushe. 1994. "Gender Differences in Marriage: Recent Research on Emotions." *Neuropsy* 9: 68–69.

Gottman, J. 1995. *Why Marriages Succeed or Fail: And How You Can Make Yours Last.* New York: Simon and Schuster.

Hatfield, E., J. T. Cacioppo, and R. Rapson. 1994. *Emotional Contagion.* New York: Cambridge University Press.

Katz, J. 1990. *Seductions of Crime: Moral and Sensual Attractions in Doing Evil.* New York: Basic Books.

Love, P. and S. Stosny. 2008. *How to Improve Your Marriage without Talking about It: Finding Love beyond Words.* New York: Broadway Books.

MacDonald, G. and M. R. Leary. 2005. "Why Does Social Exclusion Hurt? The Relationship between Social and Physical Pain." *Psychological Bulletin* 131: 202–223.

Margolin, G. and A. Christensen. 1981. "The Treatment of Marital Problems." In *Clinical Behavior Therapy and Behavior Modification,* edited by R. J. Daitzman. New York: Garland.

Maureille, B. 2002. "Lost Neanderthal Neonate Found." *Nature* 419: 33–34.

Mawson, A. R. 1999. "Stimulation-Induced Behavioral Inhibition: A New Model for Understanding Physical Violence." *Integrative Physiological and Behavioral Science* 34: 177–97.

Morrison, M. and N. Roese. 2011. "Regrets of the Typical American: Findings from a Nationally Representative Sample." *Social Psychological and Personality Science* 2: 576–83.

Rhodes, R. 1999. *Why They Kill.* New York: Random House.

Satir, V. 1983. *Of Rocks and Flowers.* Videocassette. Kansas City, MO: Golden Triad Films.

Seider, B., G. Hirschberger, K. L. Nelson, and R. W. Levenson. 2009. "We Can Work It Out: Age Differences in Relational Pronouns, Physiology, and Behavior in Marital Conflict." *Psychological Aging* 24: 604–13.

Stosny, S. 1995. *Treating Attachment Abuse: A Compassionate Approach.* New York: Springer Publishing.

Vorauer, J. D. and T. A. Sucharyna. 2013. "Potential Negative Effects of Perspective-Taking Efforts in the Context of Close Relationships: Increased Bias and Reduced Satisfaction." *Journal of Personality and Social Psychology.* 104: 70-86.

Williams, R. and V. Williams. 1993. *Anger Kills.* New York: Random House.

Wingood, G. M., R. J. DiClemente, and A. Raj. 2000. "The Adverse Sexual Health, Mental Health, and Physical Abuse–Related Consequences of Intimate Partner Abuse among Women in Rural and Non-Urban Domestic Violence Shelters." *American Journal of Preventive Medicine* 19: 270–75.

Steven Stosny, PhD, is founder of CompassionPower, a successful anger-regulation program that he has directed for more than twenty years. In addition, he has treated more than six thousand people through his organization. He has appeared on many major media programs, including several appearances on *The Oprah Winfrey Show*. He is author of *Love without Hurt* and *You Don't Have to Take It Anymore*, and coauthor of *How to Improve Your Marriage without Talking about It*. He has taught at the University of Maryland and at St. Mary's College of Maryland, and he currently has a blog on www. psychologytoday.com.

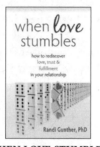

FROM OUR PUBLISHER—

As the publisher at New Harbinger and a clinical psychologist since 1978, I know that emotional problems are best helped with evidence-based therapies. These are the treatments derived from scientific research (randomized controlled trials) that show what works. Whether these treatments are delivered by trained clinicians or found in a self-help book, they are designed to provide you with proven strategies to overcome your problem.

Therapies that aren't evidence-based—whether offered by clinicians or in books—are much less likely to help. In fact, therapies that aren't guided by science may not help you at all. That's why this New Harbinger book is based on scientific evidence that the treatment can relieve emotional pain.

This is important: if this book isn't enough, and you need the help of a skilled therapist, use the following resources to find a clinician trained in the evidence-based protocols appropriate for your problem. And if you need more support—a community that understands what you're going through and can show you ways to cope—resources for that are provided below, as well.

Real help is available for the problems you have been struggling with. The skills you can learn from evidence-based therapies will change your life.

Matthew McKay, PhD
Publisher, New Harbinger Publications

new harbinger
CELEBRATING
40 YEARS

**If you need a therapist, the following organization
can help you find a therapist trained in cognitive behavioral therapy (CBT).**

The Association for Behavioral & Cognitive Therapies (ABCT) Find-a-Therapist service offers a list of therapists schooled in CBT techniques. Therapists listed are licensed professionals who have met the membership requirements of ABCT and who have chosen to appear in the directory.

Please visit www.abct.org and click on *Find a Therapist.*

For more new harbinger books, visit www.newharbinger.com